Perspectives on Prayer

Perspectives on Prayer

Edited by

FRASER WATTS

First published in Great Britain 2001
Society for Promoting Christian Knowledge
Holy Trinity Church
Marylebone Road
London NW1 4DU

British Library Cataloguing-in-Publication Data

A catalogue record for this book is available from the British Library

ISBN 0-281-05367-7

Typeset by FiSH Books, London
Printed in Great Britain by Antony Rowe Ltd., Chippenham, Wiltshire

To Bishop Stephen Verney
whose spirituality has been
an inspiration over many years

Contents

Preface

Prayer is fundamental to the religious life. It is a crucial tool by which people can become more centred on God. Yet many have too narrow a concept of prayer, with the result that their prayer life is still-born. In some ways it would be better to replace 'prayer' by a term with broader connotations, such as 'spiritual practice' – but that also has its drawbacks.

In this book, we have deliberately set out to broaden people's understanding of 'prayer'. Our strategy for doing that is to look at prayer from a variety of different perspectives. Some will be very familiar, such as, 'What does the Bible have to say about prayer?' Some are decidedly unfamiliar, such as, 'How does prayer relate to the body?' I am confident that each different perspective has its own value.

Cumulatively, I hope that the vantage-points from which we consider prayer here will expand people's concept of the nature of prayer. The exercise of thinking about prayer from the perspectives of the Bible, society, psychology, science, poetry, music, sexuality and the body can give us all a richer concept of prayer. That in turn will open up more diverse opportunities for praying. Healthy prayer needs freshness and variety, like a good diet.

This book began as a series of public lectures at the Church of St Edward King and Martyr in Cambridge, a little church that is an oasis of calm at the centre of the town. In recent years we have endeavoured to broaden spiritual practice there, and to open up the Christian tradition to spiritual seekers of different backgrounds. I am grateful to the speakers who spoke on prayer there as part of that task, and who have now prepared their talks for publication.

There are many in the Churches, and beyond them, who need the breadth of vision about spiritual practice that these chapters embody.

Fraser Watts
Queens' College Cambridge
Petertide, 2000

About the Contributors

Jeremy Begbie is Associate Principal of Ridley Hall, Cambridge and Reader in Theology at the University of St Andrews, where he directs the research project 'Theology through the Arts'. He is trained in both music and philosophy and has performed professionally as a pianist, oboist and conductor. His books include *Music in God's Purposes, Voicing Creation's Praise: Towards a Theology of the Arts*, and *Theology, Music and Time*.

Arnold Browne is Fellow, Dean of Chapel and Director of Studies in Theology of Trinity College, Cambridge. He has specialized both in New Testament studies and in counselling psychology, and has written a number of articles and chapters which attempt to relate academic study of the Scriptures to the concerns of the contemporary Church.

Charles Elliott recently retired as Fellow and Dean of Trinity Hall, Cambridge. He previously held academic posts in developmental economics in several universities, and was Director of Christian Aid. His many books include *Praying the Kingdom, Sword and Spirit, Memory and Salvation*, and *Locating the Energy for Change: An Introduction to Appreciative Enquiry*.

Denise Inge taught English for six years before embarking upon postgraduate research in Theology at King's College, London. She is presently working on a doctorate on the concept of desire in the seventeenth-century priest and poet Thomas Traherne. She lives in Ely with her husband and young daughter.

John Polkinghorne KBE, FRS, was formerly Professor of Mathematical Physics, Dean of Trinity Hall, and President of Queens' College in the University of Cambridge. He is well known for his work on the relationship between science and theology. His books include *The Quantum World*, *Belief in God in an Age of Science*, *Science and Christian Belief*, *Quarks, Chaos, and Christianity* and *Science and Theology*.

Sara Savage lectures in psychology, sociology and research methods in the Cambridge Theological Federation and is Senior Research Associate with the Psychology and Christianity Project, Divinity Faculty, University of Cambridge. Sara has been involved in using dance as a form of worship and therapy for many years. She originally trained in contemporary dance and ballet, and danced full-time for 12 years in a Christian dance company, touring widely in 17 different countries. Sara now dances with, and directs, the Christian contemporary dance group, ICON, based in Cambridge.

Angela Tilby is well known as a broadcaster and producer of religious programmes, and is the author of *Teaching God*, *Won't You Join the Dance? A Discovery of the Christian Creeds*, *Let There be Light: Praying with Genesis*, *Science and the Soul: New Cosmology, the Self and God* and *The Little Office Book*. She is a Tutor at Westcott House and has a particular interest in the life and thought of the early Church. Having been ordained in 1997, she is also a non-stipendiary minister at St John the Evangelist, Cherry Hinton, Cambridge.

Fraser Watts is Starbridge Lecturer in Theology and Natural Science in the University of Cambridge, Fellow of Queens' College, and Vicar-Chaplain of St Edward King and Martyr, Cambridge. He worked previously for the Medical Research Council as a research and clinical psychologist and is a former President of the British Psychological Society. His books include *The Psychology of Religious Knowing* (with Mark Williams), and *Psychology for Christian Ministry* (with Rebecca Nye and Sara Savage, in press), and he has edited *Science Meets Faith*, and *Christians and Bioethics*.

CHAPTER ONE

Prayer and the Bible

Arnold Browne

'We have not ceased praying' (Colossians 1.9)

Prayer and the Bible are woven together. It is a central claim of the Bible that God and humanity are related: 'He will dwell with them as their God; they will be his peoples' (Revelation 21.3). Prayer expresses this reciprocal relationship. It is encounter and dialogue, fully involving both partners, and the Bible is a record of this mutual exchange. In the Bible God speaks and is talked about, and in the Bible God is talked to and he listens. Prayer is our purposeful communication with God, and the Bible has this character of dialogue. It is the word of human beings and the word of God.

Prayer played a significant role in the formation of the Bible, and much of the material in both Old and New Testaments had its origins in worship. It is evident that some of the poetic hymns and laments of the book of Psalms played an important part in public worship in the temple and that others had their setting in private prayer. But the forms of prayer are also found in many other books of the Bible. *Celebrating Common Prayer*, the widely-used Franciscan Daily Office, collects together canticles and hymns found in more than twenty of the books of the Old and New Testaments. Songs from Isaiah, for example 'Come, let us go up to the mountain of the Lord' (Isaiah 2.3–5), recall the temple worship which sustained the prophet's vision of God as the great king of heaven and earth. The hymns from Revelation, such as 'Worthy is the Lamb that was slaughtered' (Revelation 5.12–14), evoke early Christian praise of Christ as the messianic king.

In the book of Deuteronomy, the affirmation of faith that the pilgrim is instructed to make at the harvest concludes: 'The Lord . . . brought us into this place and gave us this land, a land flowing with milk and honey. So now I bring the first of the fruit of the ground that you, O Lord, have given me' (Deuteronomy 26.8–10). This prayer moves from God's past act to his present blessings, and the speaker affirms the continuing identity of God and of his people. Similarly the account in Exodus of the first passover oscillates between past event and present observance, maintaining by worship an identity through the generations:

> You shall tell your child on that day, 'It is because of what the Lord did for me when I came out of Egypt.' It shall serve for you as a sign on your hand and as a reminder on your forehead, so that the teaching of the Lord may be on your lips; for with a strong hand the Lord brought you out of Egypt. You shall keep this ordinance at its proper time from year to year. (Exodus 13.8–10)

In the New Testament too, prayer and praise hold together the story of Jesus and the lives of Christians. The way in which Matthew records Peter's confession, 'You are the Messiah, the Son of the living God' (Matthew 16.16), or John recounts the testimony of the man born blind, 'He said, "Lord, I believe." And he worshipped him' (John 9.38), echoes the affirmations of faith of the early Christian communities: 'Jesus is Lord' (Romans 10.9; 1 Corinthians 12.3), 'Jesus Christ is Lord' (Philippians 2.11), or 'I believe that Jesus Christ is the Son of God' (Acts 8.37).

Prayer played its part in the origins of the Scriptures, and it also played its part in the process by which the biblical canon was established. When in Luke's Gospel the risen Christ says that 'everything written about me in the law of Moses, the prophets, and the psalms must be fulfilled' (Luke 24.44), the reference is to precisely the books that at that time were used in the prayers of the synagogue. The author of 2 Peter already associates the letters of Paul with 'the other scriptures' (2 Peter 3.16), and this is very probably because apostolic letters were read aloud as sermons for those gathered together for worship (see 1 Corinthians 16.21–24; Hebrews 13.20–25; 1 Peter 5.12–14). In the letter to the Colossians, which is to be 'read among you' (Colossians 4.16), prayer makes a bond between Paul, who writes that 'we have not ceased praying for you' (Colossians 1.9), and the saints in Colossae, whom he asks to 'pray for us as well' (Colossians 4.3). That the Gospels also were read in worship is clear from the evidence of Justin Martyr, writing c. AD 155 (*First Apology*, chapter 67), and the earliest surviving list of New Testament writings is concerned with books to be read in church. Indeed prayer had no less significant a role in the preservation and transmission of the biblical text as, until the invention of printing, manuscripts were copied mainly to meet the needs of worship.

The Bible cannot be considered apart from prayer. In public worship we continue to be reminded that the Bible is both the word of God and the word of human beings. We listen in the expectation that God will speak to us through the reading of Scripture. We speak, making the prayers and praises of Scripture our own, in the expectation that God will listen to us. And similarly in private prayer the Bible invites us to make its prayer our own. We can participate in that ceaseless prayer which is the continuing dialogue between the human and the divine. The Bible can be the word to which we listen and the word which we speak. It offers us the space to encounter God in prayer.

'You are God, you alone' (2 Kings 19.15)

Luke's Gospel tells us that Jesus 'would withdraw to deserted places and pray' (Luke 5.16; see also Luke 6.12; 9.18; 22.41). His teaching about prayer is consistent with this practice of often praying on his own. In the familiar parable (Luke 18.9–14), the tax collector, 'standing far off', seeks only to meet the merciful God, and indeed encounters him and is changed by him: 'this man went down to his home justified'. But the Pharisee, whose concern is essentially with 'other people', 'like this tax-collector' on whom he has his critical eye, does not meet God. Instead we are told in a colourful phrase that he was merely 'praying to himself' (verse 11). So too, in another parable in the same Gospel, a rich fool addresses his own soul, 'Soul, you have ample goods laid up for many years; relax, eat, drink, be merry' (Luke 12.19). In Jesus' Sermon on the Mount, in Matthew's Gospel, there is a similarly dramatic contrast between prayer that has only the human in view and prayer that is open to the divine:

> And whenever you pray, do not be like the hypocrites; for they love to stand and pray in the synagogues and at the street corners, so that they may be seen by others. Truly I tell you, they have their reward. But whenever you pray, go into your room and shut the

3

door and pray to your Father who is in secret; and your Father who sees in secret will reward you'. (Matthew 6.5–6)

In both Matthew and Luke, the Lord's Prayer is set in this context of Jesus' teaching about prayer. For the moment we need to note that Jesus begins with God: 'He said to them, "When you pray, say: Father, hallowed be your name. Your kingdom come"' (Luke 11.2; cf. Matthew 6.9–10). According to this pattern we do not begin with our needs, but first place ourselves within the purpose of God. In effect this is a commitment to the first commandment: 'I am the Lord your God, who brought you out of the land of Egypt, out of the house of slavery; you shall have no other gods before me' (Exodus 20.2; Deuteronomy 5.6). It is consistent with the Shema (Deuteronomy 6.4–9), which observant Jews pray each morning and evening, a practice which in rabbinic tradition represents proclaiming and accepting the sovereignty of God: 'Hear, O Israel: The Lord is our God, the Lord alone. You shall love the Lord your God with all your heart, and with all your soul, and with all your might' (verses 4–5).

It is of course the case that prayers often arise as cries for help in human need before they become songs of adoration of the divine. However, both pleas for help and songs of praise are reminders that we are not autonomous or self-sufficient, and both may serve to undermine our selfish sense of our own completeness. Solomon's prayer of dedication of the temple grounds appeals for assistance in the context of the manifestation of God's rule:

Regard your servant's prayer and his plea, O Lord my God, heeding the cry and the prayer that your servant prays to you today; that your eyes may be open night and day towards this house, the place of which you said, 'My name shall be there', that you may heed the prayer that your servant prays towards this place. Hear the plea of your servant and of your people Israel when they pray toward this place; O hear in heaven your dwelling place; heed and forgive. (1 Kings 8.28–30)

Solomon's prayer is that God may hear the pleas of those who pray toward the temple in Jerusalem, the place which represents God's rule of heaven and of earth and where his name dwells. It is similar to Ezekiel's prophecy, following the destruction of that temple, that

God will restore his people from their exile in Babylon to Jerusalem: 'It is not for your sake, O house of Israel, that I am about to act, but for the sake of my holy name' (Ezekiel 36.22).

Both Solomon's prayer and Ezekiel's prophecy anticipate the petition, 'hallowed be your name', and equally insist that prayer begins not with us but with the God to whom we pray. This same pattern is also clear in the prayer of Hezekiah, one of the few kings of Judah of whom the editors of the books of Kings approve. He is depicted praying in the temple at the time of the crisis of the Assyrian siege of Jerusalem. His plea for deliverance is grounded in his affirmation of the reality of the rule of God over his creation: '. . . you are God, you alone, of all the kingdoms of the earth; you have made heaven and earth . . . So now, O Lord our God, save us, I pray you, from his hand, so that all the kingdoms of the earth may know that you, O Lord, are God alone' (2 Kings 19.15, 19). Although we are here made aware of Hezekiah's obedience and trust, attention is focused first and foremost on God, the Creator on whose saving mercy and grace all depend.

This sense of dependence on God who creates and redeems finds frequent expression in the Psalms, as in one of the briefest:

O Lord, my heart is not lifted up, my eyes are not raised too high;
I do not occupy myself with things too great and too marvellous for me.
But I have calmed and quieted my soul, like a weaned child with its mother; my soul is like the weaned child that is with me;
O Israel, hope in the Lord from this time on and for evermore.
(Psalm 131)

The quiet voice of this woman has become the prayer of Israel. She reminds us that prayer is silence as well as words, that it is not only asking for God's action but also quietly waiting for his presence. It takes Job a long time to reach the place where this trusting mother found herself, but in the end he too declares:

'I have uttered what I did not understand, things too wonderful for me, which I did not know.
"Hear, and I will speak; I will question you, and you declare to me."
I had heard of you by the hearing of the ear, but now my eye sees you;

therefore I despise myself, and repent in dust and ashes'.
(Job 42. 3–6)

In repenting in dust and ashes, Job is acknowledging that he is content to be a human creature who cannot know the mind of the divine Creator.

In contemplating our Creator we are reconciled to our creatureliness. Without the acknowledgement, 'You are God, you alone', we will find that we are not engaging in dialogue but are praying only to ourselves.

'I knew that you are a gracious God and merciful' (Jonah 4.2)

In his letter to the Romans, Paul identifies humankind's failure to worship its Creator as the source of all that degrades and destroys: 'for though they knew God, they did not honour him as God or give thanks to him, but they became futile in their thinking, and their senseless minds were darkened' (Romans 1.21). Failing to give glory to God, human beings become their own gods, arrogant in their certainty and ruthless in their control. Refusing to give thanks to God, human beings mistake what they receive for what they deserve, and become possessive and ungenerous. They deny the truth about God and about humanity: 'they exchanged the truth about God for a lie and worshipped and served the creature rather than the Creator, who is blessed for ever! Amen' (Romans 1.25). Paul's exclamation, 'who is blessed for ever!', is at the very heart of Jewish worship. The cry 'Blessed be the Lord' is an offering to God, the song which will please him more than sacrifice (Psalm 69.30–31). Such benediction is giving thanks to God for his merciful acts, 'Blessed be the Lord, who has delivered you from the Egyptians and from Pharaoh' (Exodus 18.10). And it is glorifying him for his own sake: 'Blessed be the Lord, the God of Israel' is the triumphant climax of each of the first four books of the Psalms (Psalms 41.13; 72.18; 89.52; 106.48). Paul continues this blessing of the God of Israel (see also Romans 9.5), now blessed as 'the God and Father of the Lord Jesus' (2 Corinthians 11.31; see also Ephesians 1.3; 1 Peter 1.3). Writing to the Romans, Paul seeks to reconcile the divided community of

Jewish and Gentile Christians by inviting them to honour and give thanks to God: 'present your bodies as a living sacrifice, holy and acceptable to God, which is your spiritual worship' (Romans 12.1). Worshipping the creature, human beings are their own people, 'foolish, faithless, heartless, ruthless' (Romans 1.31), but worshipping the Creator, they are his people: 'Welcome one another, therefore, just as Christ has welcomed you, for the glory of God' (Romans 15.7). To acknowledge the truth that God is gracious and generous is to acknowledge the truth that we are created to be gracious and generous. By their praise of the God who is 'enthroned on the praises of Israel' (Psalm 22.3), the Psalms established the people's faith in the Lord as their God and in themselves as his people. So, too, the letter to the Ephesians uses the language of praise and prayer to renew the believers' understanding of God's power and purpose and of their own status as one body of Jews and Gentiles, in whom that power and purpose is at work (Ephesians 3.20–21).

Prayer reveals the truth about God and about human beings: you shall love the Lord your God and your neighbour as yourself (Matthew 22.37–39; Mark 12.29–31; Luke 10.27). We were created to be considerate, so Peter urges husbands to 'show consideration for your wives... so that nothing may hinder your prayers' (1 Peter 3.7). We were created to be righteous, and James offers the encouragement that 'the prayer of the righteous is powerful and effective' (James 5.16). But prayer reveals the truth that we are not yet what God has made us to be. Amos makes this point dramatically when he uses the form of a call to worship to denounce those who do not share the God of Israel's concern for the poor and needy: 'Come to Bethel – and transgress; to Gilgal – and multiply transgression' (Amos 4.4). Paul makes the same stark point about those in Corinth who come together to break bread, which is 'a sharing in the body of Christ' (1 Corinthians 10.16), without any regard for those in the community who have nothing. They are not waiting for the poor (1 Corinthians 11.33) any more than they are waiting for God (1 Corinthians 4.8; 15.12), and so: 'When you come together, it is not really to eat the Lord's supper. For when the time comes to eat, each of you goes ahead with your own supper...' (1 Corinthians 11.20–21).

7

In prayer and worship we discover the truth that we are not yet what we shall be. As the prayer that Jesus taught his disciples moves on from 'your' to 'our', from the Creator to the creature dependent on the gift of daily bread, so it becomes a plea for forgiveness: 'Give us each day our daily bread. And forgive us our sins, for we ourselves forgive everyone indebted to us' (Luke 11.3–4). Here too our God and our neighbour are in view, and forgiveness binds us to them both. The psalmist knew that he 'could stand' in the presence of God only because 'there is forgiveness with you' (Psalm 130.3–4). To approach God is to enter the sphere of forgiveness.

The unmerciful servant in Jesus' parable (Matthew 18.23–35), who was forgiven his debt to his master but who would not forgive his fellow slave's debt to him, entirely missed the point: 'Should you not have had mercy on your fellow slave, as I had mercy on you?' (verse 33). Jesus' command is 'Be perfect, therefore, as your heavenly Father is perfect' (Matthew 5.48), and he is 'the Lord, a God merciful and gracious, slow to anger, and abounding in steadfast love and faithfulness' (Exodus 34.6). The satirical story of Jonah has a hero who acknowledges this in his prayer, but not in his actions or his anger at Nineveh's repentance and God's mercy: 'That is why I fled to Tarshish at the beginning; for I knew that you are a gracious God and merciful' (Jonah 4.2). Whereas the pagan sailors pray to the Lord in earnest submission to his will (Jonah 1.14), Jonah's prayer reveals only his rebellion and his ruthlessness. We are left with God's concern for Jonah, 'Is it right for you to be angry?' (Jonah 4.4, 9), and for the Assyrians and their animals (Jonah 4.11).

Praying to this gracious and merciful God we may become less heartless and ruthless, and by our conversation with him may become more like him, instruments of his grace and mercy.

'Why did you ever send me?' (Exodus 5.22)

Jesus was emphatic that God wants us to pray. Although 'your Father knows what you need before you ask him' (Matthew 6.8), he is to be asked nevertheless (Matthew 6.9, 11), and will 'give good things to those who ask him' (Matthew 7.11; see Luke 11.13). Because God longs to give us what he desires us to ask for, Jesus can say: 'I tell you, whatever you ask for in prayer, believe that you have received it, and it will be yours' (Mark 11.24). God's will that we should pray is so fundamental that Jesus caricatures prayer to a generous God as persistent battering on the door of a fair-weather friend (Luke 11.5–8), or stalking an unhelpful official (Luke 18.2–5). These parables strikingly illustrate the dynamic interaction between human prayer and divine action. Persistence prods these human characters to act, as prayer produces possibilities for the fulfilment of the divine purpose.

The interaction between God and his people influences the implementation of his intentions. For those who pray 'Father, hallowed be your name. Your kingdom come' (Luke 11.2), prayer both attunes them to their part in God's loving purpose for the world and affords them the strength to perform it. This is a major theme in Luke and Acts. As Jesus spends the night in prayer before choosing twelve disciples (Luke 6.12–13), so he sends out the seventy to proclaim, 'The kingdom of God has come near', urging them to 'ask the Lord of the harvest to send out labourers into his harvest' (Luke 10.9, 2). When they return with joy he prays: 'I thank you, Father, Lord of heaven and earth, because you have hidden these things from the wise and intelligent and have revealed them to infants; yes, Father, for such was your gracious will' (Luke 10.21). Before predicting that Peter will deny him, Jesus assures him that he continues to be included by prayer in the purpose and power of God: 'I have prayed for you that your own faith may not fail; and you, when once you have turned back, strengthen your brothers' (Luke 22.32). In Acts Paul recalls the words Ananias spoke to him: 'The God of our ancestors has chosen you to know his will, to see the Righteous One and to hear his own voice; for you will be his witness to all the world of what you have seen and heard' (Acts 22.14–15). For Paul himself, prayer is central to this mission. He thanks God for the way in which the good news is received (1 Thessalonians 2.13) and the faith of Christian communities proclaimed throughout the world (Romans 1.8). He encourages those communities 'to join me in earnest prayer on my behalf' so that he may fulfil God's will by his ministry (Romans 15.30–32).

In the Old Testament too, God's servants pray effectively for others; for the implementation of God's healing and mercy. Prophets spoke for God, announcing his word of judgement and salvation, but they also spoke to God, interceding for individuals and for the nation. When the Lord listens to the voice of Elijah, praying for the life of her son, the widow of Zarephath acknowledges: 'Now I know that you are a man of God, and that the word of the Lord in your mouth is truth' (1 Kings 17.24). The people of Judah approach Jeremiah with the request, 'Pray for us to the Lord our God, and whatever the Lord our God says, tell us and we will do it' (Jeremiah 42.20), although, not liking what they are told, they decide not to do it, and suffer the consequences.

God's inclusion of his servants in the accomplishment of his will extends to his being influenced by their prayer. In promising 'I will take you as my people, and I will be your God' (Exodus 6.7), God is committing himself not to unilateral coercion but to mutual relationship. If human prayer is indeed heard 'in heaven your dwelling-place' (1 Kings 8.30), then the divine is affected by what happens on earth.

Abraham presses God on behalf of the people of Sodom, 'Will you indeed sweep away the righteous with the wicked?', and goes so far as to challenge God on his character: 'Far be that from you! Shall not the Judge of all the earth do what is just?' (Genesis 18.23, 25). And: 'So it was that, when God destroyed the cities of the Plain, God remembered Abraham, and sent Lot out of the midst of the overthrow' (Genesis 19.29). Moses too calls God to account for himself: 'O Lord, why have you mistreated this people? Why ever did you send me? Since I first came to Pharaoh to speak in your name, he has mistreated this people, and you have done nothing at all to deliver your people' (Exodus 5.22–23). Like Abraham, Moses reminds God of the demands of his reputation. He points out to God that were he to kill the people for their rebellion in the wilderness the nations would say he slaughtered them 'because the Lord was not able to bring this people into the land he swore to give them'. Moses urges: 'let the power of the Lord be great in the way that you promised when you spoke, saying, "The Lord is slow to anger, and abounding in steadfast love"... Then the Lord said, "I do forgive, just as you have asked"' (Numbers 14.15–20). Such passages reveal a God who wants us to pray because he desires to enter into a real partnership with humanity. This is the God who allows us to stand before him with our concerns, as 'Moses, his chosen one, stood in the breach before him, to turn away his wrath from destroying them' (Psalm 106.23).

'I will not let you go, unless you bless me' (Genesis 32.26)

'And do not bring us to the time of trial, but rescue us from evil' (Matthew 6.13, footnote). Jesus understood that God desires and wills our prayers, and he knew too that human beings wish and need to pray. The final petition of the Lord's Prayer is a petition for preservation. It is the basic petition of all the Old Testament prayers for help, the prayer for God's saving help in the face of any evil that may happen to us. Such cries are frequently heard in the Psalter. There are pleas for deliverance from illness:

O Lord, heal me, for my bones are shaking with terror.
My soul also is struck with terror, while you, O Lord – how long?
  (Psalm 6.2–3)

There are pleas against injustice:

Why, O Lord, do you stand far off? Why do you hide yourself in
  times of trouble?
In arrogance the wicked persecute the poor – let them be caught
  in the schemes they have devised. (Psalm 10.1–2)

At times it is right to praise the God who is present to save, but at other times the only course of honest action is to cry out to the absent God. The Psalms move between the poles of plea and praise, refusing to let go of the reality of either heaven or earth. The world's pain is lamented in the petition that it may be turned to God's praise: 'Do not let the downtrodden be put to shame; let the poor and needy praise your name' (Psalm 74.21).

If we are to accept God's invitation to partnership, then there can be no pretence. In his prayer, Jacob has the honesty to admit that he expects his piety to be to his own advantage: 'O God of my father Abraham and God of my father Isaac, O Lord who said to me, "Return to your country and to your kindred, and I will do you good" ... Deliver me, please, from the hand of my brother, from the hand of Esau, for I am afraid of him' (Genesis 32.9–11). Jacob then resumes his own strategy to appease Esau, but on his way he encounters the stranger at Jabbok with whom he wrestles. This is the very God he had tried to control with his prayer and now seeks to overpower with his strength, still insisting on his blessing: 'I will not let you go, unless you bless me' (Genesis 32.26). This is a meeting between the real Jacob and the true God, a mutual struggle in which neither is overcome. Jacob is blessed and he is changed. As he moves on limping because of the struggle, so he moves forward broken of his habit of control and towards reconciliation with his brother. His prayer for deliverance has been answered in an encounter which has made him open to the love of God and of his neighbour.

'Amen. Come, Lord Jesus!' (Revelation 22.20)

The first Christians were swift to make the connection between their prayers and the prayers of Jesus. We know that it was not long before the Lord's Prayer was established as a congregational prayer for Christians, and the different versions in Matthew and Luke preserve the wording handed down in two communities in which it was prayed.

In the Gospel of Matthew, Jesus' prayer is presented to the Jewish Christians for whom the Gospel was written as an example of prayer (Matthew 6.9–13). Matthew's community first learned to pray as children, and the brief and focused Lord's Prayer, which is contrasted with the 'empty phrases' and 'many words' of the Gentiles, recovers a directness which may be dulled by a familiar routine.

In Luke's Gospel, Jesus' prayer is presented to the Gentile Christians for whom this Gospel was written as a model prayer (Luke 11.2–4). Whereas, as we have seen, the Hebrew Scriptures portrayed conversation with God on the analogy of conversation between humans, Greco-Roman prayers in this period tended to be formalized and lengthy, with a concern for exactness of performance and wording. Matthew's Jewish Christians were schooled in prayer, but Luke's Gentile Christians needed to learn to pray. In Luke's Gospel it is by observing Jesus' own practice of prayer that the disciples are led to ask him about it: 'He was praying in a certain place, and after he had finished, one of the disciples said to him, "Lord, teach us to pray, as John taught his disciples." He said to them, "When you pray, say: Father, hallowed be your name. Your kingdom come"' (Luke 11.1–2). The reference to John the Baptist teaching his disciples is a reminder that religious groups were characterized by their particular prayers, and it suggests the early importance of the Lord's Prayer to the identity of the Christian community. Possibly Paul's use of 'Abba! Father!' (Romans 8.15; Galatians 4.6), where the Aramaic appears alongside the Greek, is a recollection that Jesus had addressed God in this way and taught his disciples to do the same. Certainly both Matthew and Luke show us that, whatever their circumstances, Christians learned from the Lord's Prayer how to pray.

We have seen that Luke stresses the constancy of Jesus' praying, particularly at critical moments – at his baptism (Luke 3.21), in choosing the twelve (6.12), at his transfiguration (9.28), and in Gethsemane, where, says Luke, 'in his anguish he prayed' (22.44). The letter to the Hebrews also preserves the memory of Jesus' prayer as anguished struggle: 'In the days of his flesh, Jesus offered up prayers and supplications, with loud cries and tears, to the one who was able to save him from death, and he was heard because of his reverent submission' (Hebrews 5.7). This recalls Gethsemane, where Jesus' prayer acknowledges that deliverance can only be through fulfilment of the will of God: 'Abba, Father, for you all things are possible; remove this cup from me; yet, not what I want, but what you want' (Mark 14.36). It recalls also the cry from the cross, 'My God, my God, why have you forsaken me?' (Psalm 22.1, quoted in Matthew 27.46 and Mark 15.34). Lamenting with the psalmist, Jesus identifies with him in holding together suffering in the absence of God with the hope of his presence: 'But you, O Lord, do not be far away! O my help, come quickly to my aid!' (Psalm 22.19).

For his followers it is Jesus' death and resurrection which hold together the absence and presence, the suffering and the hope of Psalm 22. As the dying Jesus used the psalm in his lament from the cross, so the letter to the Hebrews puts it on the lips of the risen Christ proclaiming the good news of God's salvation: 'I will proclaim your name to my brothers and sisters, in the midst of the congregation I will praise you' (Psalm 22.22, as quoted in Hebrews 2.12).

Jesus' prayer brought together God and humanity in the promised reciprocal relationship. His earthly prayers for humanity, 'Father, forgive them; for they do not know what they are doing' (Luke

23.34) are one with his prayers in heaven, 'since he always lives to make intercession for them' (Hebrews 7.25; see Romans 8.34; 1 John 2.1). And so Christians join their prayers with his, praying in his name (e.g. John 14.13; 15.16; 16.23–24), or 'through Jesus Christ' (e.g. Romans 1.8; 5.11; 7.25; 16.27). This is the prayer of the Spirit within, which draws us into that reciprocal relationship realized in Jesus: 'When we cry, "Abba! Father!" it is that very Spirit bearing witness with our spirit that we are children of God' (Romans 8.15–16).

Amen! is a response which is both praise of God, in acknowledgement of the truth of his word, and offering of self, in acceptance of its claim on us. The book of Revelation acclaims Jesus as himself 'the Amen' (Revelation 3.14), and Paul also explores this theme: in Jesus Christ, 'every one of God's promises is a "Yes." For this reason it is through him that we say the "Amen", to the glory of God' (2 Corinthians 1.20).

Prayer as dialogue with God is above all prayer as participation in the death and resurrection of Christ: 'for as all die in Adam, so all will be made alive in Christ' (1 Corinthians 15.22). Amen! Come, Lord Jesus!

Further Reading

Balentine, S. E., *Prayer in the Hebrew Bible: The Drama of Divine–Human Dialogue.* Fortress Press, Minneapolis, 1993.

Brueggemann, W., *The Psalms and the Life of Faith.* Fortress Press, Minneapolis, 1995.

Cullmann, O., *Prayer in the New Testament: With Answers from the New Testament to Today's Questions.* SCM Press, London, 1995.

Miller, P. D., *They Cried to the Lord: The Form and Theology of Biblical Prayer.* Fortress Press, Minneapolis, 1994.

Ryrie, A., *Silent Waiting: The Biblical Roots of Contemplative Spirituality.* Canterbury Press, Norwich, 1999.

CHAPTER TWO

Prayer and Society

Charles Elliott

This chapter falls into three parts. I shall start by asking what we think we are doing when we pray for society. That will lead me into a more existential account of the integration of prayer and living-in or being-part-of society. I shall conclude by taking more specific account of the corporate or community-based nature of public prayer.

When we pray for society either as individuals or as members of a worshipping community, we are likely to become acquainted with three styles or types of prayer for social concerns. The fact that to describe them is simultaneously to reveal their crudity is merely a demonstration of how hard we find it to incorporate genuine compassion for wider society into our existing models of formal or even informal prayer.

The first model we are familiar with might be called, with only modest burlesque, the 'shopping list'. 'Hot spots' (e.g. East Timor, Mozambique, Ethiopia) are mentioned and commended to the Lord without much detail or analysis or expression of intent in anything but the vaguest terms. One is often left with a sense of deep unease by this kind of prayer. What precisely are we doing? Reminding God? Showing him that we care? Expressing some kind of solidarity with the victims? I will come back to this later, but for the moment let me say at once that I fully recognize that this may be the best we can do. For all its ambiguity and seeming inadequacy, bringing to mind the suffering of the world with a few carefully chosen but thinly sketched allusions may be the limits of what is available to most of us. The shopping list may be faintly comical and can easily become absurd: but that should not lead us to condemn it out of hand.

The second model we know well is the 'news bulletin'. This is, by definition, more extended, more topical, more detailed than the shopping list, and, especially as it is deployed in public worship, often feels like a subterranean way of bringing the congregation up to date and reminding them of material the prayer leader thinks they ought to know about. This confusion of information or education with prayer can be distracting for people more used to a meditative or contemplative style of prayer; and may not actually encourage many people in the congregation to move out of the informational, heady bits of themselves into a deeper encounter with God or with genuine suffering. If part of prayer is com-passion – and I take that to be so foundational that it needs no more explication – then a style of praying that makes compassion more difficult to engender may not be serving the praying needs of the congregation well, whatever it may be doing for their informational needs.

The third model I call the 'hair shirt' model. I call it that because it has the effect – which may or may not be consciously intended by the prayer leader – of inducing guilt. The guilt may be because we are comfortable and 'they' are not: that is the most primitive type, and arguably the least helpful. Or it may be because the congregation is being reminded of their own collusion or complicity in the processes that have brought about suffering elsewhere. Let's ignore the first and concentrate on the second, for there is an interesting dynamic at work here. There is a sense in which we are all caught up in many of the processes that create and maintain world poverty, social exclusion, armed conflict and the denial of human rights in many parts of the world. Most Western Christians deny this, and many are deeply offended when they are reminded of it, especially in church. (I recently elicited a rafter-shaking snort of outrage from the Master of a Cambridge College by sketching out – in a sermon rather than in public prayer – the effects of the forty-year decline in the terms of trade of developing countries. It is considered below the belt to refer to such facts in an ecclesiastical building; though it would be considered a serious dereliction of duty to ignore them in the lecture hall next door.) Now whatever the pathological theology at work here, we need to be clear about what the prayer leader is seeking to achieve by inducing guilt in the praying community – when they have very little if any opportunity to change their ways. If they could stop the arms trade or remove brutal kleptocrats from office or help bring up the unwanted children of single mums on sink housing estates, then there would indeed be pastoral and perhaps prayerful point in bringing about a crisis of conscience out of which real behavioural change might flow. But to assume that is to confuse structural categories. Most of us are pawns in other people's games and, although we are not innocent bystanders, we are nonetheless powerless bystanders to what is done in our name (or more often without any reference to us at all). As I have argued elsewhere, this combination of guilt and powerlessness is peculiarly seductive – but also peculiarly destructive. And perhaps it is most destructive of serious prayer, precisely because the more guilty we feel without the possibility of change in the circumstances of our guilt, the more painful it is to wrestle at depth with the issues at all. Better to turn our attention to something, however trivial, that we can do something about.

Perhaps even worse, I fear that this guilt-inducing model contains within it, or invites as a reaction to it, a kind of spiritual dishonesty. It encourages a bogus form of repentance; a repentance of the lips that cannot be worked out in the fabric of everyday life. We are now in deep water, because it could well be argued that any kind of repentance is better than no awareness of the need for repentance – and there is real power in that argument. I cannot, however, pursue it further here; but must settle for stressing that this is a difficult and potentially dangerous area. Those who use intercessory prayer for the wider world in a way that leaves people feeling guilty and unable to 'amend their lives' should, I suggest, at the very least be aware of what they are doing, and the dynamics they may well be releasing. They might also want to ask themselves whether guilt and powerlessness are emotions that move people to a deeper level of prayer. I suggest they are only rarely. For most people they are an invitation to disengage – or even, worse, to move into a sublimated blaming of God for the kind of world he has made or permits to exist. And that is, at the very least, an unhelpful approach to prayer.

If these are the three styles of prayer for the world that one often encounters in public worship, and, equally, in one's own private prayer, we need to ask what difference we think we are making. We presumably think we are seeking to change the world; but are we seeking to change God's mind about the world? There are clear resonances of this style of thinking in the Old Testament and even in Jesus' own prayer – for example, in Gethsemane. (Jesus is bending his will to that of the Father, but he holds out the possibility of the Father changing the content of that will.) We need to step with reverent caution here. It is inconceivable that God is indifferent to the plight of, say, HIV children in rural Africa. It is inconceivable that he needs us to remind him of the horror of that plight. It is inconceivable that he wills anything other than their highest good. So why does he need our prayers? It is hard to avoid the conclusion that the point of prayer is to change our minds and hearts, rather than God's. Yet that seems a little too simple, a little too glib (though, as we shall see, certainly not unimportant).

There is a sense, I believe, in which prayer – real, sincere, persistent prayer – changes the externals, makes things happen, in a way that is qualitatively different from changing the mental or spiritual states of some of the actors. I know that such a view is currently unfashionable. I know that many scientists, including some Christian scientists, would want to emphasize the randomness of creation. They would appeal to theories of chaos. I understand both the theological and the existential difficulties of thinking that prayer does do something to God. Yet, the Christian witness through the centuries, and certainly the witness of modern saints, is that there is a sense in which pathways open up to make benign change possible seemingly as a result of faithful prayer by faithful people, a possibility not excluded by John Polkinghorne in his contribution to this volume.

The nearest analogy is to spiritual healing. There is plenty of evidence, although it is, again, random, incoherent, inconsistent and difficult to handle, that sometimes healing takes place seemingly as a result of prayer either by a specially gifted individual or, perhaps, by particularly committed communities. It doesn't seem to me to be too big a leap to move from the healing of the individual body to the healing of the social body. There are all kinds of analogies between individual health and social health. If, in our own experience, we sometimes think that prayer makes a difference to the way that the chemical and neurological pathways of an individual body work, is it then too fanciful to think that there are occasions –

unpredictable but real – when prayer makes a difference to the way that the social pathways of the corporate body function? In that sense prayer has clearly achieved something which otherwise would have been impossible, and therefore one would want to say that prayer has shifted something that is directly or indirectly part of God's providence.

I would like to focus now more on the main actors for good and for evil. Again, think of East Timor, or of Northern Ireland, but as you do that, think too that there are good and not very good actors in each one of us. Again, I would want to draw a parallel between the individual and society. Do we believe that prayer can reinforce the psychic good in the personality of people involved in a particular situation or, similarly, do we think that prayer can undermine the psychic evil in people involved in a particular situation? Is there some sort of transference of psychic energy which changes the balance of good and ill in the key actors? I don't know. The evidence is, again, extremely fragile and difficult to handle.

But my own personal experience is that people in very tight corners – people in emergency situations in the third world, people in dangerous, difficult, life-threatening, life-consuming situations – again and again, and often to their own great surprise, report how they have felt supported, encouraged, enabled. The way they describe the experience, time and again, is to say, 'It was as though some invisible force or power was sustaining me.' However fanciful and irrational that might seem, I can only report that people have said that to me many, many times in situations in which they have been at their wits' end. If they report that they have felt some invisible power at work giving them energy and courage they didn't know they had, and you know that there have been communities of faithful people praying for them on a sustained basis, you can deny the relationship of cause and effect, but I think you have to be careful how you handle the evidence. In the end, of course, it does require a leap of faith to attribute inner courage to external (and distant) support. I can only say that, for myself, I have seen it and heard it so often, that I am as convinced as I need to be that, in some way that I do not pretend to understand, there is a relationship between a praying people and the people they are praying for.

Finally, are we changing ourselves as we pray about social issues?

Here it is easier to answer with an unqualified 'Yes'. Prayer does change us, and the more imaginative and disciplined and persevering the prayer, the more likely we are to be changed. This reinforces the well-known aphorism that prayer is a dangerous activity. If you really pray, you may find yourself being changed in all sorts of ways that you had not foreseen. I want to identify four ways in which we may find ourselves being changed.

The first is an increase in compassion and empathy for the people we are praying for, or even an increase in en-joyment with people for whom we are giving thanks or celebrating. We are drawn into their reality by processes of memory, imagination, and by reconstituting the reality we are praying about within our own consciousness.

Second, at a deeper level, we are changed because we are sharing something of God's reaction, God's horror, or God's joy. If you want to put it in slightly medieval terminology, it is as though we are drawn nearer the heart of God and therefore enabled to share in what is going on in that heart. Finding ourselves nearer the heart of God is inevitably going to change us, possibly in the deepest sense of convert us.

Third, prayer in this sense has a revelatory quality, because we often become aware of the subtle liens that bind us into the situation we are praying about. You cannot pray legitimately about East Timor and remain careless of the part that British arms trade with Indonesia has played in that disaster. You cannot pray responsibly for Northern Ireland and remain careless of the shameful history of English involvement in that country. In that sense, we cannot any longer maintain a safe distance from what we are praying about. We are drawn into it and find, often to our surprise and our shame, that individually, or, more likely, corporately, socially and even ecclesiastically, we have to accept our share of collusion with destructive forces.

Fourth, and most obviously, prayer will often inspire us to action. Maybe prayer will even shame us into action. Can you really pray about homelessness and not buy a magazine such as *The Big Issue*, that supports the homeless? To anticipate a theme to which I shall return presently, there is a mutual integrity-check operating here. If my behaviour is not brought closer to gospel values, maybe my prayer is not as heartfelt nor honest nor committed as I imagined.

And if my prayer lacks spiritual bite, maybe one reason is that it has become divorced from the realities I see around me.

So far most of my illustrations and applications have implied crisis situations. That is too limiting. For I want to say that every social event, every social relationship – whether it is going shopping, going to a party, going to a meeting, having a chat in the street – every social activity is the stuff of prayer. Shopping is a good example. Shopping is an activity we all undertake day by day, week by week, that tells us so much about ourselves and about our society. Have you ever tried making a shopping expedition a meditative act of prayer? To see God in what you buy and what you don't buy, to see God in how you choose, to see God in the faces of your fellow shoppers, in the face of the checkout person? It is only when we begin to open our social selves to that kind of transformation that we begin to draw God into the stuff of our daily lives.

This notion of God in all things, including the supermarket trolley, including the television programme, including the cocktail party, is deeply Johannine and even Pauline: Paul uses the wonderful phrase of the whole creation 'groaning' for its liberation. It is also deeply eucharistic. Maybe we should have a Eucharist in the aisles of the local supermarket; maybe we should have a Eucharist in a restaurant. Maybe that is the way that we need to relate our thanksgiving, not to some ethereal area of discourse 'out there', but to the world incarnate. Maybe it is when we find Christ stacking the shelves or serving the soup that we become aware of the divine indwelling in a way that would be literally revolutionary (and very familiar to Eastern Orthodoxy).

Let me try to earth that. Recently I spent a day in London's Wandsworth prison. As I walked through the litter-strewn, grim little courtyards or looked up at the razor wire, with bits of textile and paper and garbage clinging to it, or walked the corridors or looked into the tiny cells and saw prisoner after prisoner sitting on their beds, staring into space, a voice within me kept saying, 'Where is God in this? What is God doing here? How do I make this experience of the people at the bottom of society into an act of prayer?' I am still wrestling with that. When I go back to that prison, I shall look for and find humanity and, very occasionally, acts of compassion from the prison staff. I shall look for and find humour

21

and courage and desolation and shame and guilt, and I shall be wanting to make of those a tabernacle, a tent, in which God can be seen to dwell.

During my visit, I had a conversation with a very serious sex offender with a lengthy sentence. He was telling me how awful life in prison is. He was recounting brutality by the staff, injustice by the governor, appalling bullying by fellow prisoners. I have no means of telling if he was speaking the truth, or fantasizing, or exaggerating, and I was not there to judge that. Eventually I said something like, 'Is there anything you have encountered here that you really value?' As I asked the question, I thought to myself, 'How do you have the nerve, after all that he has told you, to ask such a crass question? If he has any sense he'll throw you out.' But he said, 'Yes. The woman who comes in to teach us yoga fills the space with her presence and her calm.' He went on to give me a moving account of what learning to meditate in the tradition of yoga has meant to him. It has made prison tolerable and has changed the parameters of his life.

I began then to see that God is moving in the prison, not just in the person of the woman who teaches yoga, but in every conversation that prisoner has with his fellow prisoners, in every moment in which he is able to withdraw from the horror of that place and discover something of the beauty and goodness of God. For me that was a moment of the deepest prayer, of thanksgiving, of joy, of offering, of beauty, because here was a man who, having committed a dreadful crime, was being changed beyond recognition not by his own efforts, but by a grace beyond him. In the process he was able to change others by a grace beyond them. I offer this story to you as a kind of parable, or image, of what prayer in society, prayer about society, prayer for society, might be for each of us.

As we have seen, praying for society can be an individual or a corporate activity. In most Christian traditions, with the possible exception of some charismatic-fundamentalist churches, there is a tradition of public prayer for society, often expressed in Erastian circles as prayer for the Monarch and government; perhaps more focused on the victims of social processes in the various independent or dissenting traditions. In either case, the church as a community prays for the wider community of which it is a special, 'called-out', component. We need to pause for a moment to ask what is involved in being a praying community. What is the nature of the spiritual transactions that are happening when one (ecclesiastical) community prays for another (secular) community?

There is, of course, a long established literature on this from the point of view of the monastic vocation. One of the primary purposes of the monk or nun is precisely, under most Rules, to be fully available as an intercessor for the world. No one can read the works of, or on, Thomas Merton, for example, without becoming aware of how central is this vocation – and, incidentally, how independent of 'head' knowledge about what is going on in the world it can be (in marked contrast to at least two of the models above). While recognizing that whole strand of the Christian experience, however, I want to look at the more widespread phenomenon of the local Christian community devoting itself to prayer, perhaps in the course of common worship, for society. I want to raise three questions. What is the relation between the social bonds in the community and the integrity of its prayer for wider society? What is the nature of leadership in public prayer for society? And finally, what is likely to happen to a community that takes prayer for society seriously? I will examine those questions in turn.

The first question can be expanded like this: Is it the case that a divided, embittered, self-centred congregation prays less often, less fervently, less 'effectively' for society than a harmonious community in which the fruits of the Spirit are abundantly evident? At first sight, one would be tempted to answer in the affirmative, for how can a bitter people produce sweet prayer? Unfortunately both the biblical tradition and the experience of the Church makes no such easy assumption tenable. And a moment's reflection suggests why that may be so. If the people of God are – and, at least at some level, know themselves to be – far removed in their own experience from what God is calling them to be, they are likely to identify more effectively with both the victims and their oppressors in the wider society. In that sense the experience of failure as Church is an invitation to a more heart-felt engagement with the experience of failure as secular community. But the parenthesis above is important. A complacent and complaisant Church that is unaware of the poor quality of its corporate life cannot, by that very unawareness, make the necessary connections between its own difficulties with living together in a truly gospel way and the wider society. Hence the huge – but much resented and even hated – role of the internal critic, the prophet who points out the shortcomings of the social relations of the people of God. Jeremiah is not the only one such to end up at the bottom of a well!

The second question is about the nature of leadership in corporate prayer for society. This is a narrow way in to a much larger question: the role of ideology in forming the social construction of social reality; and therefore the social construction of the vision towards which prayer might be directed. The prayer of a church co-opted by a vicious regime – Pinochet's Chile in its worst years – is likely to be very different from the prayer of a church heavily influenced by, say, the early writers in the liberation theology tradition. Those extreme cases are easy to see; and almost banal to explore further. The issue becomes more interesting in the fuzzy middle, typically inhabited by most churches in the United Kingdom. In such an environment there is no necessary commitment to a well-articulated or obvious political ideology; but that does not mean that there are no ideological presuppositions. There nearly always are; indeed some would argue that they are a necessary precondition of any kind of rational understanding of the universe in which we operate. The issue then is to see by what means those political ideological assumptions are subjected to theological critique. A moment's reflection, however, will remind us that there can be no watertight distinction between the two. How we read our theology will be influenced, and at the margin determined, by how we read the 'real' world. In common with many others, I have tried to explore these relationships a little further elsewhere. Here I will only add that though there are no easy solutions, a necessary first approach is to be aware of the problem. To put it in more pious language, as we lead corporate prayer for society, we need to be aware not only that we do not see the world in exactly the same way as other people in the community; but also that our perspective is inevitably partial, distorted and incomplete, falling far short of the loving gaze of God. In so far as we are capable of correcting the distortions of our ideologically determined construction of the world – and that is for most of us most of the time an open question – obviously we hope to shift them in the direction of the ultimately loving perspective of

God. That is a work of grace, dependent finally on the activity of the Spirit.

The third question was about what happens to a community when it takes prayer for society seriously. There is no one answer to that, and the assumption that prayer for society inevitably results in a high level of social engagement, for example on the model of the Sojourners in the USA, is disproved by many a monastic community that takes prayer for the world very seriously but stays within the bounds of its Rule of life which precludes any overt engagement. There is, however, the danger of being misled by the exceptional: for most secular congregations most of the time, the expectation has to be the same as we saw for individuals: that disciplined prayer moves the praying community to action. In the case of the community, however, there is an additional bonus to be looked for beyond the integration of inner life and outer life. As Bonhoeffer among many others often emphasized, the integration of corporate outer life and inner life, in the sense above, has an effect on the discovery of the praying people as community. And that surely accords with our experience: that when people pray together and work together to implement a small part of their prayers, they discover a level of trust, mutual respect and mutual support that did not exist before. To say that is not, of course, to deny that it can all go horribly wrong, nor to imply that integrated prayer-and-action is any kind of guarantee against the spiritual and emotional ills that can afflict any community. (Bonhoeffer's own context should warn us against that.) Nonetheless, the gift of God to his people as they struggle to be more faithful is surely a deepening awareness of what it means to be the Body of Christ in a particular social and political context.

And that is a good note on which to end. For it does not seem to be inconsistent to claim that prayer for society can hold together three dynamics which are at the heart of the Christian life because they are at the heart of God. The first is the movement of the Christian – individually and corporately – towards God. That movement is basic to any kind of prayer and is emphatically not excluded by the fact that the object of our prayer is secular and 'this-worldly'. The second is the movement of the Christian soul from self to suffering-others. If the bane of much private devotion is a kind of spiritual narcissism, the cure is the empathetic holding-up of the suffering of the world to a God who dies for it. And the third is the movement of the individual pray-er, in love and possibly in action, towards fellow Christians embarked on the same enterprise. These three dynamics interplay, interweave and vary in intensity and priority over time and between people and communities. It is when one is too much neglected that prayer for 'the world' becomes insipid, routinized or absurd. Normally, the corrective is to go back to basics: to concentrate on the first dynamic, and allow that to set the pace and context for the others. For the music of the spheres and the inarticulate groaning of creation are not, after all, as far apart as we might imagine.

Further Reading

Cobble, J., and Elliott, C. (eds), *The Hidden Spirit: Discovering the Spirituality of Institutions.* Christian Ministry Resources, 1999.

Elliott, C., *Praying the Kingdom: Towards a Political Spirituality.* Darton, Longman & Todd, London, 1985.

Elliott, C., *Memory and Salvation.* Darton, Longman & Todd, London, 1995.

Graham, E. L., *Transforming Practice: Pastoral Theology in an Age of Uncertainty.* Mowbray, London, 1996.

Gutiérrez, G., *We Drink from Our Own Wells: The Spiritual Journey of a People*, tr. M. J. O'Connell. Orbis Books, New York, 1984.

CHAPTER THREE

Prayer and Science

John Polkinghorne

Can a scientist pray? How someone answers that question will depend upon what sort of prayer they have in mind. For myself, I think many scientists pray prayers of adoration without knowing that they are doing so. As physicists study the physical world, they are greatly impressed by its rational beauty and order. Paul Dirac, who was one of the founding fathers of quantum theory, and who was not at all a conventionally religious man, said that his life had been spent in a quest for beautiful equations. It was by using mathematical beauty as his guide that Dirac was able to make his great discoveries. 'Wonder' is an indispensable word in the vocabulary of a scientist, to describe the deep satisfaction that from time to time rewards our researches, as the marvellous order of the world is revealed to our enquiry. It is not difficult to see this experience of wonder as expressing worship of the Creator, whether consciously acknowledged as such or not. In Free School Lane in Cambridge, upon the archway that leads into the Old Cavendish Laboratory, passers-by can see inscribed in Latin the verse from Psalm 111 that says 'The works of the Lord are great, sought out of all them that have pleasure therein'. The text was put there by James Clerk Maxwell, the first Cavendish Professor and one of the greatest physicists of all time. I am glad to say that when the Cavendish laboratory moved to new buildings, the then Cavendish Professor, Nevil Mott, made sure that the same message greeted the visitor on arrival.

However, the question of a scientist's relationship to prayer becomes much more challenging when it is petitionary prayer that we have in mind. After all, science seems to describe a universe that is very regular and orderly in its workings. Previous generations might pray for rain in times of drought but 'amen' may well stick in the throat of many if such prayers are offered in church today. Doesn't the weather just happen? We no longer think of rain as the opening of the heavenly water sluices, but simply as the result of the operation of the great heat engine of the Earth's seas and landmasses.

Yet the God of our Christian faith is a personal God. When we use such human language about the divine, we know that it is being used in some kind of stretched or analogical sense; but if personal language about God is to mean anything at all, surely it must imply that God does particular things in particular circumstances. We call God Father rather than Force because we believe that the divine care does not operate automatically, like the force of gravity, but in response to individual need. There is a great deal at stake for Christianity (and I believe for Judaism and Islam too) if we can answer 'Yes' to the question, 'Can a scientist pray a petitionary prayer in a way that is positive, without impugning his or her scientific integrity?'

One might think that the way to cut the Gordian knot of this theological perplexity about God's providential action would be simply to appeal to divine omnipotence. After all, can't God just do what God likes? It is important to recognize what we mean when we say that God is 'almighty'. Of course, in one sense God can indeed do what God likes, but God will only want to do what is in accord with the divine nature. The very last thing that the utterly consistent and rational God can be is a kind of capricious celestial conjurer. Love works by process, respectful of the independence and integrity of the other, and not by an overruling magic. This means that in the act of creation, God has graciously given to creation the gift of being itself, in its own due independence. We can think of an evolutionary world as a creation that, in a famous phrase, is 'allowed to make itself'. Moreover, the very laws of nature, whose regularities are discerned by the scientist, are to be understood by the theologian as being willed by God and as reflecting the divine faithfulness. God does not work against these laws of nature, for that would be the theological nonsense of God working against God. If God acts in the world, then, it will be within the grain of the universe and not against it.

28

Of course, divine consistency is not at all the same thing as dreary uniformity. It is the consistency of a person and not of a force. In unprecedented circumstances, totally unanticipated things may happen, giving rise to those events which, because of their unexpected character, we might call miracles. Such happenings are to be understood as insights into a deeper divine rationality than we are ordinarily able to discern. That is why St John calls Jesus' miracles 'signs'. It is similar to the way in which unanticipated physical phenomena, such as superconductivity, are insights into deeper consequences of the laws of nature than we had previously appreciated. Yet miracles, by their very nature, are going to be rare events, triggered by exceptional circumstances. In our prayers we are concerned with something more everyday – what the theologians call 'special providence' – rather than an out-and-out miracle like the resurrection.

If God works within the grain of nature, we have to ask whether that grain is, in fact, sufficiently open to accommodate these actions of particular divine providence, without arbitrary disturbance. In a mechanical universe, such as people in the eighteenth and nineteenth centuries believed the world to be, that could hardly be the case. If the cosmos were a gigantic piece of clockwork, then the only role for God would be the deistic one of the Great Clockmaker, who had constructed the machinery, wound it up, and now just lets it tick away. One might well admire such a wonderful machine, but one would just have to hope that it worked out all right. There would be no point in asking for something different, unless one thought that God was an interfering deity who might be persuaded occasionally to poke a divine finger into the works, itself a notion with severe theological difficulties.

We have always known, however, that the world is not merely mechanical, for we know, as surely as we know anything, that we are not just elaborate pieces of clockwork. In the eighteenth century, people wrote books with titles like *Man the Machine*, but they never believed their writings to be no more than the scribblings of an automaton. To do so, would have been to saw off the rational branch on which they sought to sit as they framed their argument. There must be more than mechanism.

Twentieth-century science has, in fact, seen the death of such a merely mechanical view of the universe. Two blows have finally finished it off. One was the discovery of quantum theory, the astonishing fact that the physical world is cloudy and fitful at its subatomic roots. The quantum world is unpicturable and unpredictable in its behaviour. Fascinating as this discovery is – and I have spent a great deal of my adult life working as a quantum physicist – I do not think that it is of the highest significance for our present topic. When we talk about prayer, we are talking about events in the everyday world which involve the behaviour of trillions of atoms. Although each atomic event has some degree of randomness in it, the variations tend to cancel each other out in the combination of huge numbers of such events, and so to produce an overall pattern of great reliability. It is the same effect that the Life Insurance Offices depend upon to make their money. They do not know when a particular person will die, but the actuaries have a very good idea about what proportion of people in that kind of group will die in the next five years, because again the individual uncertainties cancel each other out in the behaviour of the whole. I doubt very much that God acts principally in the world by scrabbling around at its subatomic roots.

Much more significant, I believe, for our present purpose is another surprising discovery of twentieth-century physics that has only been properly appreciated in the last 40 years or so. It relates to the physics of the everyday world, the physics that would have been familiar to Sir Isaac Newton and which we usually call classical physics. It shows that this kind of physics has consequences that Isaac did not anticipate and which would have surprised and interested him very much.

Those of us who learnt classical physics did so by considering certain simple systems, such as a steadily ticking pendulum. These systems are tame and robust. By that I mean that if you disturb them a little, the consequence for their behaviour is correspondingly slight. They are predictable and controllable – in a word, they are mechanical. We thought that all the everyday physical world was like that, but we now know that, though there are some Newtonian clocks, most of it is made of clouds. By that I mean systems that are so exquisitely sensitive to circumstance that the smallest disturbance will produce large and ever-growing changes in their behaviour. It will scarcely surprise anyone to learn that one of the ways in which this behaviour first came to light was through the study of models of the weather. Ed Lorenz was trying to simulate the behaviour of the Earth's weather systems. To his great surprise, he found that the slightest variation in the input to his simplified equations produced exponentially growing deviations in the behaviour of their solutions. In the trade, this is called 'the butterfly effect': a butterfly stirring the air with its wings in the African jungle today could produce consequences that grew and grew until they produced a storm over East Anglia in about three weeks' time. Since we cannot possibly know about all those African butterflies, long-term weather forecasting is never going to work!

This is such an astonishing discovery that I would like to try to explain it a little more. For an example I shall take the air in a room. As we know, it consists of lots of little molecules whizzing around. They are not exactly billiard balls, but the way that they collide with each other can be modelled sufficiently accurately by treating them as if they were. These molecules are fast moving and quite close together, and so in a minute fraction of a second they have many collisions with each other. After only 50 such collisions we could not calculate accurately whether one of these molecules would be moving towards the back wall or away from it without having to take into account the effect of a single electron (the smallest particle of matter) on the other side of the observable universe (about as far away as you can get) interacting with the molecules in the room through the effect of gravity (the weakest of the fundamental forces of nature). That is the degree of sensitivity that is involved. How it comes about is as follows. Newton himself solved the problem of how to calculate the collision of two billiard balls. It is precisely determined provided you know exactly the angle at which they impact on each other. However, the angle at which they separate is very sensitive to the angle at which they collided. As anyone who has played snooker knows, a slight error in cueing produces disastrous and frustrating consequences for the subsequent shot. That is for one collision. In a sequence of 50 collisions, these effects multiply exponentially, producing this extraordinary sensitivity. Here we have a cosmic butterfly effect with a vengeance. We cannot possibly know about all those distant electrons, so that as simple a system as the air in a room is intrinsically unisolatable, and unpredictable in its detailed behaviour.

The discovery of the existence of these very sensitive systems has been given the name of the theory of chaos. Unfortunately, it is not aptly chosen, for it turns out that their behaviour is not completely random but it has about it a kind of ordered disorder: there is a pattern to their haphazardness, which is called 'a strange attractor'. Chaos theory is therefore a kind of oxymoronic subject. I now want to ask what significance we should attribute to its discovery.

All agree that chaotic systems are intrinsically unpredictable in their behaviour and unisolatable in their character. Yet, at least as originally mathematically formulated, this apparently random behaviour originates from the extreme sensitivity to initial conditions of the solutions of perfectly deterministic equations. Is then the lesson to be learnt that apparent haphazardness may disguise underlying determinism, or is the situation so strange that it calls for some radical reinterpretation? If the latter strategy is followed, the original deterministic equations will have to be understood as being approximations to some more subtle and more supple kind of theory.

An interpretative choice of this kind is a metaphysical decision, going beyond science itself in making a decision whether to accord greater significance to the equations or to the behaviour. One may put the issue this way. Unpredictability refers to what philosophers call epistemology, what one can know. We cannot know in detail the future behaviour of a chaotic system. Is this fact to be interpreted simply as a matter of unavoidable ignorance, or is it a pointer to there being an actual openness in the future behaviour of these systems? The latter claim would concern what philosophers call ontology, what is actually the case (as opposed to what we can know about it, which is the concern of epistemology).

Scientists are instinctively realists; that is to say, they believe that what we can know is a reliable guide to what is the case. If we did not think that in science we were learning what the physical world is actually like, why should we submit to all the weary and demanding labour involved in scientific research? My wife once gave me a sweatshirt emblazoned with the stirring slogan 'Epistemology models Ontology'. I believe that realist conviction to be the natural metaphysical stance for a scientist.

How this attitude works out can be illustrated by a celebrated incident in the history of quantum mechanics. Heisenberg showed that, in quantum theory, it is not possible to measure absolutely accurately both where an electron is and how it is moving – in physics terms, one could not know both its position and its momentum. This is Heisenberg's famous uncertainty principle, and it was obviously initially an epistemological result about our ability to know. Within a very short time, however, Heisenberg and almost all other physicists were interpreting it ontologically, as a principle of indeterminacy. It wasn't, in their opinion, simply that you couldn't know an electron's position and momentum; it just didn't have either position or momentum until you measured one or the other. For them, epistemology modelled ontology.

I wish to adopt the same strategy in relation to chaos theory and to draw the metaphysical conclusion that the everyday world is more subtle and more supple than a mechanical universe (Polkinghorne, 1998). Added confidence in this approach is fostered by the recognition that it would, in its abolition of the deterministic, offer a glimmer of hope to physics of being able to describe a world of which we could conceive ourselves as being inhabitants. (We have already recognized that we are not automata and it is a gain for science if it achieves a picture open enough to accommodate this fact.)

Working out what this could mean is necessarily at present a tentative and speculative exercise. To say that the future is open does not mean that it is a kind of whimsical lottery, but rather that there are causal principles, over and above the conventional physical picture of exchanges of energy between constituents, that help to bring it about. Since chaotic systems are unisolatable, we should expect these new principles to be holistic in character, relating to the totality of what is happening and not to the individual component parts. The future behaviours of a chaotic system (the portfolio of possibilities called its strange attractor) all have the same energy but they differ in their patterns of behaviour. Therefore, we may expect the new causal principles to be concerned with the specification of pattern rather than the input of energy. Putting these notions together leads to the idea of causality of a top-down kind (the influence of the whole upon its parts), exercised through something one might call 'active information' (a principle of pattern formation). It all begins to have a glimmer of similarity to our experience of agency, the bringing about of our intentions by the action of the whole person.

Of course, these ideas are speculative, as ideas about the nature of agency necessarily are for us today. I think that they have some value, though I have to issue a warning that by no means everyone agrees with me. Nevertheless, I want to take seriously this option for describing physical processes of an open kind. It seems to me that if the world has this character that permits us to act as agents within it, then it is also possible for us to believe that God acts providentially within its open grain as well. As embodied beings, we obviously act both energetically and informationally. God, a pure spirit, will, I believe, interact with creation through the input of pure information. If there is any truth in these ideas, it is possible for a scientist to pray with complete integrity, in the belief that God is indeed providentially causally interactive within the unfolding open history of creation.

Some interesting consequences follow from this point of view:

1. God's action will always be hidden within the cloudy unpredictabilities of chaotic regimes. Providence may be discernible by faith, but it will not be demonstrable by experiment. It will have the character of benign coincidence, rather than the exercise of naked power. It will not be possible to itemize history, saying that nature did this, human agency did that and God did the third thing. All are inextricably mixed together.

2. Although there are many clouds, there are also quite a lot of clocks. For the believer, their regularity will be a sign of the Creator's faithfulness. Long ago, in the third century, the great Christian thinker, Origen, recognized that there are some things that one should not pray for, such as the cool of spring in the heat of summer (however tempting that might be in Alexandria, where Origen lived). The succession of the seasons is a clockwork part of terrestrial experience and the faithful God will not set it aside for human convenience.

3. The picture I have given is one of an open future in which both

human and divine agency play their parts in its accomplishment. Christian theology must always seek to find a middle way between two extreme and unacceptable pictures of God's relationship to creation. One is that of the Cosmic Tyrant, who brings about everything by divine will alone. The universe created by the God of love cannot be a divine puppet theatre, but instead creation is allowed to be and to make itself. This gift of creaturely freedom has its cost, for it carries with it the implication of a degree of precariousness in what happens, due to the self-restriction of divine control. Not everything that occurs will correspond to God's will. Neither the act of a murder nor the incidence of a cancer are in accordance with the Creator's good intention, but they are allowed to happen in a creation given its independence. However, this does not mean that God is just an indifferent spectator of what is going on, for that would be the other theologically-unacceptable extreme view. We have to seek a middle way in which there is divine interaction with creation without there being divine tyranny. The balance needed corresponds to a cosmic version of the celebrated theological problem of the balance between grace and free will. I believe that the picture I have set out is capable of accommodating this middle way.

When a scientist prays, he or she knows that they are not just filling in a blank cheque written for them by a heavenly Father Christmas. There are great mysteries in the operation of divine providence and the divine responses to prayer (Polkinghorne, 1989). Not only are there the clashes of human desires – the vicar praying for a fine day for the church fête and the farmer praying for rain for the crops – but there are also the deeper strangenesses of individual human destiny. Bishop Ian Ramsey told the story of two men crossing the plains of North America in a covered wagon in pioneer days. They are set upon by an Indian band and a hail of arrows descends upon their vehicle. The horses are whipped up and they make an escape. One of the men has survived the attack but his partner has been killed. Ramsey rightly says that if the survivor is to speak of God's providence in his escape, he must also be prepared to speak of God's strange providence in the death of his friend. There is no facile way of understanding these mysteries. After all,

Christianity has a cross at the heart of its story.

A friend of mine was diagnosed as having terminal cancer. His doctors gave him six months to live. It was all a great shock. My friend and his wife were both devout Christians and they were advised to pray together every day, seeking God's healing. Of course, many others of us were praying for them too. My friend died almost exactly six months to the day from the time that he had been given the diagnosis. Afterwards his wife asked herself what had been the fruit of their prayers, and she was generous enough to share her thoughts with us. She concluded the following: her husband was someone who had faced a lot of opposition in the community in which he lived. However, even his strongest opponents were deeply impressed with the courage and fortitude with which he faced death and this led to the healing of rifts in that community. He had a condition that could have led to a distressful death, but in fact he died peacefully at home. His wife concluded that this was the healing that had been granted in response to prayer. No doubt, they had been hoping for something different – some physical remission – but they were able to accept God's will in the form of their sad destiny.

One might go on to ask, why should we pray at all? If God is good, why are we not given what we need without having to ask for it? What is going on when we pray? Are we persuading God to do something that otherwise wouldn't happen if we hadn't made a fuss about it? Are we drawing the divine attention to something that otherwise God would have overlooked? Or are we suggesting a rather clever plan that God would not have thought of unaided?

Obviously none of these things can possibly be what is going on in petitionary prayer. In fact, I think we are doing two things when we pray:

1. I have given a picture of how the future comes about, in which there is some power resulting from human agency and God has reserved some power for the exercise of providential agency. I suggest that when we pray we are offering our room for manoeuvre in bringing about the future to be taken and used by God, together with the divine providential room for manoeuvre, to produce the greatest possible good effect. In more

conventional language, we are seeking to align our wills with the divine will. I believe that the interrelational character of reality means that such an alignment can have consequences for third parties also. A metaphor I often use is that of laser light. What makes such light powerful is that it is, as the physicists say, coherent. That means that all its waves are in step, so that crest coincides with crest, trough with trough, adding together to produce the greatest possible effect. In incoherent light, crest and trough can coincide and cancel each other out. In prayer we are seeking a laser-like coherence between human and divine wills and that can be genuinely instrumental and it can bring about consequences that would not be possible if these wills were at cross-purposes. This idea has two implications. Prayer is not a substitute for action but a spur to it. If my elderly neighbour is lonely, I do not deal with that simply by staying at home and praying for them. I have to be prepared from time to time to pay a visit, even if it means hearing yet again those too familiar stories about the old days. The second implication is that corporate prayer is a good thing. We tend to feel that this is so, but why should it be? Because there are then more fists beating on the heavenly door to gain divine attention? Obviously not, but because there are more wills to be aligned with the divine will to bring about God's good purposes.

2. I owe my second understanding of what petitionary prayer is all about to John Lucas (Lucas, 1976). Lucas says that when we pray we are called upon to commit ourselves to what it is that we really want. In other words, we are given the opportunity to assign value and such an assignment will be taken seriously by God, though, naturally, not as an absolute obligation because we might be badly mistaken. I think this is right, and it is both helpful and also challenging to us to be serious about our requests. In the Gospel, a blind man comes to Jesus and stands before him (Mark 10.46–52). The Lord then says, 'What do you want?' For heaven's sake, it's clear what he wants. He's a blind man; he wants to see. Nevertheless, he has to commit himself, to say 'My teacher, let me see again', before he is healed. In a similar way, we have to commit ourselves to what it is that we really want, to what is our heart's desire. Prayer is a very serious business.

Can a scientist pray? Yes, I think he or she can with integrity and trust and, of course, many do, for many of us scientists are also religious believers.

References

Lucas, J. R., *Freedom and Grace*. SPCK, London, 1976.

Polkinghorne, J. C., *Science and Providence*. SPCK, London, 1989, especially Chapter 6.

Polkinghorne, J. C., *Belief in God in an Age of Science*. Yale University Press, London, 1998, especially Chapter 3.

Further Reading

Gleick, J., *Chaos*. Heinemann, London, 1988.

Polkinghorne, J. C., *Science and Providence*. SPCK, London, 1989.

Tracy, T., *God, Action and Embodiment*. Eerdmans, Grand Rapids, 1984.

Ward, K., *Divine Action*. Collins, London, 1990.

CHAPTER FOUR

Prayer and Psychology

Fraser Watts

In this chapter I will examine the human side of prayer, the mental and emotional processes of people that engage in prayer. I am not suggesting that prayer can be reduced to these psychological processes, or that it is 'nothing but' psychology. In considering the benefits of prayer, there are always two sides to consider. First, there are fundamental theological assumptions about the God from whom those benefits come. Second, there is the human side of how those benefits are mediated. These are complementary aspects of the study of prayer, each illuminating a different aspect of it. This chapter will explore the human side of how the benefits of prayer are mediated.

Even at a human level, belief in God makes a crucial difference to how people approach prayer. It is hard for people to pray to God for specific things in a heartfelt way if they are not sure whether or not there is a God. They may be able to meditate equally well, but it is perhaps one of the crucial differences between prayer and meditation that prayer presupposes belief in God whereas meditation does not. My personal position, let me be clear, is that there is a God to whom we pray. However, it is not my purpose here to try to argue for the existence of God, I will simply assume it.

In looking at the human processes by which the benefits of prayer are mediated, some people are inclined to say that these human processes are all there is to prayer. However, there is no need to conclude that. The fact that there are psychological processes involved in the benefits of prayer does not in any way mean that those human processes are entirely responsible for its benefits. To put it at its lowest, it is equally possible that there is a real God with whom people are in communion when they pray, but that communion with him is mediated and experienced through the same psychological processes as we experience everything else.

This issue is likely to come into increasingly sharp focus as we come to understand more about how the physical brain is involved in prayer. At present, we understand a good deal about brain processes in meditation; much less about their role in prayer. However, it is probably only a matter of time before our scientific knowledge of that improves. The important question is how such knowledge should be interpreted. Some will no doubt say that the benefits of prayer arise solely from certain specific brain processes. However, it is again perfectly plausible that the benefits of prayer flow from the God to whom people pray, but that they are mediated through the physical brain. There is no reason why God should bypass the physical brain which is part of his creation.

In looking in detail at the human side of prayer, it will be helpful to look at the psychological and religious dimensions of different forms of prayer such as confession, thanksgiving, petition and intercession, adoration and praise.

Confession

The prayer of confession raises a difficult problem, which is often a concern in the religious life, namely what view should be taken of guilt. In the twentieth century there seems to have been a conflict between the religious and the psychological worlds on the question of guilt.

Many psychologists have drawn attention to the negative aspects of guilt, how it can become excessive and irrational. The degree of guilt people feel is sometimes quite out of proportion to what they have done. People can come to have an irrational tendency to feel guilty about almost anything at all, regardless of their degree of culpability. Such guilt can be depressing and debilitating. Many psychologists have, understandably, seen the task of therapy as being to liberate people from such forms of guilt.

The churches have generally differed from psychologists in their view of guilt. At almost every church service there is an act of confession, often with very abject language in which it seems that we are being asked to express quite extreme guilt and remorse. Some preaching has also been designed to make people feel guilty about the way that they live, as a way to encourage them to repent and remodel their lives – though that is more true of preaching in previous generations than the present one. The Church seems to have used guilt as an important tool in the Christian life.

The way to resolve these apparently opposing views of guilt is to distinguish between different kinds of guilt. Excessive and irrational guilt, as the psychological community has rightly pointed out, is dangerous and harmful. Not all guilt, however, is excessive and irrational. It is appropriate to feel guilt in proportion to wrong we have done.

Psychology can provide ways of understanding unpleasant emotions such as anger and guilt. It is unlikely that we would have such negative feelings if they served no purpose. Their function is to help us to identify when things are going wrong in our lives, to act as an alarm, a signal that we need to reorient our goals and desires. Guilt is one of these negative emotions which inform us of when our plans need to be realigned. Thus, contemporary theories of emotions, like Christian teachings before them, have come to recognize that some forms of guilt are functional and valuable.

These observations have practical application when it comes to the prayer of confession. Such prayer should not be seen as an occasion to wallow in excessive feelings of guilt. A prerequisite of confession is discerning what it is that we should really be confessing; to see where our actions have done harm to ourselves or others. Confession is an opportunity for self-appraisal, discernment and penitence, but not just for abject guilt.

Those who criticize the emphasis placed on guilt within the Church often fail to acknowledge that appropriate guilt and penitence lead on to absolution and forgiveness. The central reason for the act of confession is not to encourage people to wallow in guilt, but to allow them to receive absolution and forgiveness. It is not always easy, however, to receive forgiveness. The obstacles are similar to those encountered in psychotherapy. Early in the process of psychotherapy, people often arrive, at an intellectual level, at the key insights that will be central to their therapy. However, there is often a long way to go before what is called 'effective insight' is attained, in which these insights are deeply understood and truly accepted in a way that helps people to change the way they think and live. Taking hold of the assurance of forgiveness is a similar process. Intellectually believing one's sins are forgiven is quite different from really receiving that forgiveness. There can be a long work of reflection involved in taking forgiveness on board, just as there is before intellectual insights become effective insights in the course of psychotherapy.

The formal sacraments of the Church can sometimes be helpful in this process of accepting forgiveness. It may make more impact on someone who is racked with guilt to make their confession to a priest individually. Having told the priest what is really on their conscience, to hear a specific declaration of absolution directed at them personally, in full knowledge of what they have done wrong, may make more impact than a general confession and absolution in the context of a church service.

Thanksgiving

It is a natural human instinct to be grateful when things go well in our lives. In some ways the prayer of thanksgiving is like saying thank you to God for the good things in our lives, as we would thank a friend for a nice gift. But it is much more than that. As St Paul said, we should give thanks to God for everything, in all circumstances (see 1 Thessalonians 5.18). In this way, thanksgiving to God is quite unlike ordinary thankfulness. If we think of the prayer of thanksgiving as being simply the act of thanking God for the nice things, then we have not understood what is really involved.

Psychologists have been interested in the last two decades in what they call 'attributions'. 'Causal attributions' are causes assigned to events in one's life. People differ in an interesting way in how they attribute causes to events, such as when they are thinking about their successes and failures. Some people take failures personally, others may write them off as due to external factors. There is a tendency among some people to take a rosy view of themselves, seeing successes as a reflection of their true ability, and writing failures off as being due to external factors or the unfairness of the world. But there is also a depressive view of life in which failures are attributed to one's own inherent lack of ability, and successes are attributed to chance or undeserved good fortune.

Each of these selective patterns of attribution has unhelpful psychological consequences. The rosy view inclines people towards inappropriate confidence or arrogance. On the other hand, a negative pattern of attributions can lead to debilitating depression. We need to be liberated from taking either successes or failures too personally. Giving thanks to God for what happens in our lives provides an opportunity for such liberation from excessive pride on the one hand, or excessive shame and depression on the other.

Learning to give thanks to God for everything can be a transforming and liberating experience. It can liberate us from egotism, from simplistic distinctions between what is good and bad in our lives, from shallow and narrow-minded attitudes to adversities. St Ignatius talked about moments of 'consolation' in the religious life; not the nice times, but the times that bring us close to God. It challenges our usual mindset to ask, not whether events are merely pleasant or enjoyable, but, more importantly, whether they bring us closer to God. The prayer of thanksgiving is an opportunity to rethink our lives in this way.

There are some things that it is especially difficult and challenging to give thanks to God for. There is much evil and suffering in the world and in our lives. How are we to give thanks to God for these? God does not will or cause suffering and adversity; neither is he detached and uncaring about it. Rather, the God in whom Christians believe is a God who is deeply involved in the world and cares about suffering and adversity. He is there with us when we suffer. But he is also a God who allows the world freedom and independence; he does not step in and interfere with events in a way that overrules our freedom. He influences the world chiefly through influencing the people in it, rather than by directly intervening in nature in a way that bypasses human agency. We have the opportunity to co-operate or not with God, to respond to his invitation or to ignore it. We thank God for everything in our lives because he is with us in adversity and wishes us to join him in overcoming it and in bringing good out of it.

There is a sense in which God is always responsible for what happens and it is always appropriate to give thanks to God. However, that does not preclude ourselves or other people being involved and responsible too. In framing causal attributions, we should beware of asking whether it was God on the one hand, or ourselves on the other, who was responsible for something. God does not influence events in the same way as human beings. So, giving thanks to God does not imply that human beings do not carry their share of responsibility as well.

Petition and Intercession

There is a certain immediacy and directness about coming to God in petition, and asking for the things that we desire. It is also a form of prayer that raises a dilemma: what sort of thing should we ask for? At one end of the spectrum we might ask for the things we most want for ourselves – material possessions, a better job, or the ideal partner. At the other end of the spectrum we might ask what we think we ought to be asking for, such as humility, moderation or virtue. Neither of these extremes is very helpful. The reason that the prayer of petition is helpful at a psychological level is that it is a tool for the transformation and purification of our desires. If it is to work in that way, we need to bring God the things we actually desire. There is then an opportunity for those desires to be transformed in the presence of God.

I am making the theological assumption that all our desires are capable of being transformed and redeemed, even desires of which we might feel ashamed. Some of our desires, in their 'raw' form, may indeed be unworthy or shameful. However, it is an assumption of the Christian faith that such desires can be transformed and redeemed in the presence of God.

I am also making a psychological assumption, that we do not have perfect knowledge of our own desires. Often when we get what we thought we desired, it is strangely unsatisfying. For example, people who have won large amounts of money on the National Lottery may find that, although their desire to be rich has been fulfilled, happiness still eludes them. It is often the case that if our fantasies become realities they are not quite what we had hoped. This is because we do not understand our own desires very well. Our real needs would give us deep fulfilment if they were met. The gulf between desire and fulfilment is a challenge to go beneath what we think we want, to find those things that would really give us fulfilment. The prayer of petition gives us an opportunity to do just that; to reflect in the presence of God on what we really need and desire.

There is a way of probing beneath our superficial desires that is used in some forms of cognitive therapy, called 'chasing down'. It is a process that is similar to what can be done in the prayer of petition. To take an example, a couple might come for marital therapy. The therapist would, using this technique, ask each of them to name two or three things they would really like to ask for from the other. One of them might ask that their partner would stop getting drunk, or going out with his or her friends so often. It is then helpful for the therapist to probe beneath these requests by asking each partner why they want what they have asked for, and what it means to them. This leads to a deeper level of desire. With each new level of desire, the therapist can 'chase down' what lies behind it, until fundamental needs and desires are revealed. This is similar to the process by which our desires can be purified in the presence of God in the prayer of petition.

Confession, thanksgiving and petition are all forms of prayer that start from where we are in our own lives. There are other forms of prayer that more explicitly take us outside ourselves, and whose value derives from the fact that they do so. Intercession is one of these; in intercession we ask for things, not for ourselves, but for other people. Thus intercession has a capacity to lift us out of our egocentricity and give us a wider perspective. It can challenge us to understand more deeply what other people's needs are (just as the prayer of petition challenges us to understand our own needs more deeply). It calls for a degree of empathy and sensitivity to what other people truly need, rather than merely what they or we think they need. It can lead to a deeper understanding of those we care for. Praying for someone else's needs can transform our relationship with them. If we are feeling irritated or fed up with someone, for example, there are few things that can transform that more effectively than praying for them.

Adoration and Praise

Of all forms of prayer, adoration is the form that focuses most explicitly on God, and his unlimited glory, majesty and graciousness to us. The prayer of praise and adoration, like the prayer of intercession, has the psychological benefit of lifting us out of ourselves.

Praise also lifts us out of our normal judgemental mindset. We live in a world in which procedures of appraisal have become commonplace. Everyone these days is being appraised and making appraisals. Though there is a place for close and thorough appraisals of how well we are each doing, it can also be helpful to lift our minds and hearts out of all that. The psychological value of giving praise to God is that he is the one being to whom we can fittingly give unlimited praise. It is not only right and proper that we should give such praise to God, it is also psychologically liberating for us to open our hearts in an act of unstinting appreciation.

The worship of God can sometimes sound repetitive, but that does not mean it is insincere (though it can be). In its repetitiveness, it is rather like two lovers saying again and again how much they mean to one another. Once that has been said a few times, it ceases to be informative, and there is no real communication value in saying it again. The reason why lovers go on expressing their love is not that the other person doesn't know it already, but that they find it a joy to go on saying it. The worship of God is rather similar. God does not need to be told what we think of him. The point is that he invites the praise of him that is fitting because it does us good to offer it.

Meditation

Most of this chapter has been about reflective, active and cognitive forms of prayer, but the prayer of silence is also extremely important. Many people in our society are seeking some sort of meditative practice. It is one of the tragedies of Christian ministry in recent decades that so many people who have looked for meditation have thought that the Christian Church had nothing to offer them, and have gone elsewhere for it. There are deep meditative riches in the Christian tradition, but we have tended to hide that light under a bushel. It is very important for Christian churches to let people know that you can learn to meditate there.

One of the key things that is required in meditation is to learn a kind of stillness in both mind and body. Most of us are very distractible; our minds flit from one thought to another. In our complicated lives, we have ever-shorter attention spans. It is sometimes useful to be able to switch our attention rapidly from one subject to another, but is also quite stressful to spend all our time doing so. It is immensely valuable and liberating to be still and to focus on something simple for an extended period of time.

Meditative stillness is not easy to achieve, but with patience and perseverance it becomes easier. It also helps to meditate in the company of other people; most people find it easier to remain still and undistracted when meditating with others. The key principle in dealing with distractions is to be patient and gentle, and gradually the capacity for stillness will grow. One key principle is not to struggle over it, which simply makes things worse. The right approach is captured beautifully in the advice Augustine Baker gave to the people to whom he was spiritual director in the seventeenth century (Baker, 1964). He advised someone who was troubled by 'sinful or pernicious' thoughts to 'quietly divert his mind' from them. There may also be a way of using the distracting thought as a cue that leads back towards the subject of meditation.

Meditation also involves the stilling of emotions, something about which there have sometimes been psychological concerns. Freud was exercised by the dangers of people suppressing their feelings. He saw the danger of some feelings being so unpleasant that people were unable to admit them into consciousness, and considered such bottled-up emotions to be psychologically unhealthy. There is a difference, however, between stilling one's emotions in meditation and suppressing them. Meditation does not involve being unaware of your feelings; it involves allowing your feelings to take a gentler form, in which you can be more attentive to them and less overwhelmed by them. It is rather like tasting a fine wine: to taste it well you drink just a little; you do not get drunk on it. If you want to understand your emotions well it is often best, similarly, to pay attention to them in a restrained and moderate way, rather than to give them free reign.

The concept of 'emotions' is a term that only came into widespread use in the second half of the nineteenth century, under the influence of the emerging scientific psychology of figures including Charles Darwin and William James. Before that time, in Christian thinking about the soul, people had made a distinction between the 'passions' and the 'affections'. Roughly speaking, 'passions' are emotions that have run riot and are out of control, whereas 'affections' are gentler emotions that can help in the process of discrimination and spiritual purification. Meditation helps both to control the passions of the soul, and also to attend to one's gentler affections in a clearer and more discriminating way. There is no suppression of emotions involved in meditation.

Meditation also helps us to look at the world in fresh ways, and to look at it with a new kind of directness. We can see this most clearly when people meditate on some physical object that is in front of them. There are some classic psychological experiments by Arthur Deikman in which people came into rather a bare room that just contained a blue vase (Deikman, 1966). They were asked to concentrate all their attention on the blue vase, not to think about it, but just to focus on the colour, shape and form of the vase. When doing this, people experienced some quite surprising and interesting things. The shape of the vase dissolved in some cases; for others its colour became more intense; often, subjects felt that the vase was coming towards them; for others, the boundary between themselves and the vase dissolved. It is suggested that these experiences were akin to the experiences of the classical mystics, such as the author of the great medieval text, *The Cloud of Unknowing*. There are perhaps only limited similarities, but they are interesting. Learning to focus attention in stillness on a simple object in a non-discursive way helps people to see things in a new way.

Of course discursive knowledge is of great practical usefulness, and there is no suggestion here that such knowledge should be devalued or abandoned. But people also need the still, attentive mode of knowing that meditation can teach. There are both psychological and religious claims to be made about the importance of meditative forms of attentiveness and insight. Meditation helps to still our minds and our passions, and helps us to recover from the hurly-burly of life. In meditation, we can centre ourselves in a way that we cannot when we are discursively thinking around things, and switching our attention from one object to another. There is a lot of empirical evidence that transcendental meditation brings considerable psychological benefits.

Meditation is also particularly valuable in a religious sense. It helps us, in the words of Elijah, to 'be still and know God'. God is not a being that we can get to know through thinking around him in a discursive kind of way. It is helpful to do that sort of theological reflection at times, but we do not come to know God himself that way. Meditative attention to God, focusing on simple images such as the cross, or the flame of a candle, or a simple scriptural text, can lead us to know God in a way that no amount of discursive thought can ever achieve.

Different Ways of Praying

It is important to emphasize that there are many different ways of praying. For example, prayer changes as children grow up. However, at present psychologists can tell us more about how children's understandings of prayer develop than about how they actually pray. The main focus in children's prayers seems to be on petition, and a gradual change can be seen in what they pray for. As they grow up, their prayers are increasingly constrained by moral and spiritual considerations. For example, they only pray for what they think they ought to pray for. Also, their ideas change about how God answers prayer.

It is more difficult to generalize about how adults pray. They are extremely diverse, and pray in different ways in different circumstances. On occasions, most adults revert to praying urgently in a child-like way, for what they most need. In evolving a proper integration between urgent, heartfelt prayer and more constrained, edifying prayer, it may be helpful for people to pray in both ways at different times.

Perhaps the most important issue about adult prayer is how far people are really engaged in it, as opposed to simply 'going through the motions'. The most helpful way of conceptualizing this from a psychological standpoint is in terms of how far the whole person is involved in prayer. Prayer that is only an intellectual activity, or a public performance, fails to engage the whole person. In contrast, prayer that engages feelings and has implications for action is clearly engaging the person more holistically. Prayer is one of the interesting contexts in which we can observe the difference between 'cold' and 'hot' cognition, between emotionally engaged and emotionally detached ways of thinking. There is a similar distinction in psychotherapy between clients who explore their problems in a merely intellectual way and those who do so with full emotional engagement. It is the latter kind of exploration that has implications for subsequent action.

There has recently been some fruitful thinking about the relationship between different types of personality and ways of praying. The main focus for this has been the Myers Briggs Type Indicator (MBTI), which uses Jung's classification of personality types. There is room for scepticism about exactly how neatly people can be classified into personality types, and also about how adequately the MBTI assesses personality. Also, there is probably no neat mapping of personality type on to ways of praying. Nevertheless, the Jungian distinction into sensing, intuitive, thinking and feeling types has opened up a fruitful exploration of the diversity of prayer. It also raises in an interesting way the question of the balance between praying in the way that comes naturally and learning to explore other forms of prayer that do not come so easily. There seems to be value in both. The psychological study of how different kinds of people pray promises to continue to be a fruitful way of exploring the rich diversity of prayer.

Conclusion

I have offered here an overview of the different forms of prayer and their psychological and religious value, looking at confession, thanksgiving, petition and intercession, adoration and meditation. In each form of prayer there is clear psychological value, and an opportunity for real personal transformation. There is no doubt that prayer can have considerable value to the person who prays. But, to repeat the point with which I began, I am in no way saying that prayer is 'nothing but' a psychological process. I believe there is a real God into whose presence we come when we pray, and who is the agent of the transformations prayer brings. I have simply tried to describe here, in human and psychological terms, how it is that prayer works its benefits within us.

References

Baker, A., *Holy Wisdom*. Anthony Clarke, London, 1964.

Deikman, A., 'Deautomisation and the Mystic Experience', *Psychiatry* 29 (1966), pp. 324–38.

Further Reading

There are chapters on the psychology of prayer in:

Watts, F., and Williams, M., *The Psychology of Religious Knowing*. Cambridge University Press, Cambridge, 1988; reissued by Geoffrey Chapman, London, 1994, Chapter 6 (meditation) and Chapter 8 (prayer).

Lee, R., *Psychology and Worship*. SCM Press, London, 1955, Chapter 5.

The fullest treatment of the psychology of prayer is in:

Brown, L., *The Human Side of Prayer*. Religious Education Press, Birmingham, Alabama, 1994.

On meditation see:

West, M., *The Psychology of Meditation*. Oxford University Press, Oxford, 1987.

For a Jungian approach to prayer see:

Ulanov, A., and Ulanov, B., *Primary Speech*. SCM Press, London, 1985.

There is now an extensive literature on prayer and personality type, see for example:

Duncan, B., *Pray Your Way: Your Personality and God*. Darton, Longman & Todd, London, 1993.

For a classic study of children's understanding of prayer, see:

Goldman, R., *Religious Thinking from Childhood to Adolescence*. Routledge & Kegan Paul, London, 1964, Chapter 12.

Books of a more philosophical kind that are relevant to the psychology of prayer are:

Phillips, D. Z., *The Concept of Prayer*. Blackwell, Oxford, 1965.

Brummer, V., *What Are We Doing When We Pray?* SCM Press, London, 1984, especially Chapter 2.

CHAPTER FIVE
Prayer and Poetry

Denise Inge

'Prayer' and 'poetry', the two title words of this chapter, rest easily together. In terms of intellectual and spiritual seriousness, they are equally weighty. Six letters each, they look well on the page, poised perfectly either side of their nondescript conjunction. They even alliterate. Each names an entire world of language and silence, waiting and words, of attentiveness. What could be nicer? And yet, it was not always so.

I would like to begin in the late sixteenth and early seventeenth centuries, that period at 'the confluence of the Renaissance rhetorical tradition and Reformation theology' (Clarke, 1997, p. 1) since, in some sense, those are the beginning years of the uniquely Anglican tradition in the United Kingdom, the tradition in which I find myself, in terms of my own belief and practice. In the first part of this chapter I will look at the struggles of some of our early divine poets to find an authentic divine/poetic voice. I will also look at the climate which necessitated that struggle, and at two examples of the work they produced. Then I will jump several hundred years to our own age with its very different premises and concerns, broadening out the discussion from the divine poem itself to the wider use of poetic language in worship and public prayer, what one might call the poetics of modern theology and liturgy.

Picture yourself in a Puritan age poised for truth, simple and plain – and Poesie, the province of pagans and lovers, the language of erotica and idolatry, the stage and the bedroom. Couple with that the 'rime mars truth' notion of the sixteenth and seventeenth centuries, which demanded plain speaking and decried adornment, and you may have some sort of idea of what I am trying to suggest. Poetry was not for theologians.

As Elizabeth Clarke notes in her recent study, *Theory and Theology in the Work of George Herbert*, the great Tyndale, in his debate with Thomas More (1528–33), 'used the word "poet" as a term of abuse' (Clarke, 1997, p. 1). 'There was universal concern that preoccupation with the "husk" of words could divert attention from the "kernel" of truth.' Richard Rogers, in his *The Practice of Christianitie* (1618), scorned those who 'preferre the Case before the Instrument, the Rinde before the Pith' (quoted in Clarke, 1997, p. 1).

There is, of course, the poet Philip Sidney, with his great works such as *Arcadia* and *A Defence of Poetry*. But here too, he is striding out against the tide. Sidney's *A Defence of Poetry*, it is thought, was a response to criticism from Stephen Gosson in his *Schoole of Abuse*, dedicated to Sidney in 1579. Such a work as Gosson's was not unique. The late sixteenth century saw many books and pamphlets being published that attacked literature in general, drama in particular, and, by association, poetry as well (Clarke, 1997, p. 2). And the public demand for such material was great – emotive titles from the erudite such as *Treatise Wherein Vain Plays or Interludes are Reproved* to the sensational *A Mirror of Monsters* spanned several decades.

But public opinion was only one of the formative pressures felt by writers of poetry. The king's favour was another. What the king liked mattered. And when his predilections changed, that change was reflected in the writing of the time. There was an increase in the appearance of published verse during the early years of James I (Sylvester, cited in Clarke, 1997, p. 3), but by about 1610, as one critic notes, 'straight theology without poetic embellishment was perceived as the best way to attract the king's attention and favour' (Doelman, 1994, p. 35).

Evidence of this trend can be seen, for example, in the work of Joseph Hall and William Leighton. Leighton, who had received a knighthood for the publication of his 1603 *Virtue Triumphant*, felt the need to begin his 1613 volume with an apologetic declaration of intent (Clarke, 1997, p. 4). Joseph Hall, bishop of Exeter and Norwich, contrasts his 1607 paraphrase of the Psalms with his earlier 1603 volume *The Kings Prophecie* characterizing this later work as 'holy and strict' (Hall, 1949) and then spends the rest of his preface in argument in favour of religious poetry. The main elements of his argument are (1) scriptural precedent, (2) the effectiveness of poetry and (3) that his poetry is deliberately simple. Hall was clearly aware that even this paraphrase of the Psalms, scriptural though it undoubtedly was, would lay him open to the possibility of censure. He writes in a letter to a friend, 'I have boldly undertaken the holy meeters of David... there is none of all my labours so open to all censures' (Hall, 1949, p. 271). Similarly, Giles Fletcher wrote, in his preface to *Christ's Victorie and Triumph* (1610) 'Some... thinke it halfe sacrilege for prophane Poetrie to deale with divine and heavenly matters' (quoted in Clarke, 1997, p. 4).

Clearly, although there are biblical precedents for poetry, particularly in the Psalms and the Song of Songs, many poetic writers of the late sixteenth and seventeenth centuries felt the need to defend or apologize for their work. Poets, then, were not above reacting to the prevailing wind of their day, whether it be the personal likes and dislikes of their king or the popular voice published in Puritan tracts. In the seventeenth century, divine poets were in defensive postures. Let us look at one such poet, Lady Southwell.

Lady Southwell was known to have participated in the manuscript circulation culture of the court in which one writer passed his or her work on to the next, commented, made puns, wrote replies to it, and so on. It was an economy of wit entered into by Donne, Herbert and many others. In fact, Lady Southwell herself played word games with Donne and was published in 1614 in a work which gives evidence of this. This particular poem is taken from 'Precept 4':

> To lay fair colours on a wrinkled hide
> Or smooth up vice with eloquent discourse
> Who writes for pence, be he so turpified
> And let those nine Chimeras be his nurse
> > To teach him to crawl the Heliconian hill
> > and in Parnassus dip his ivory quill.

> For me, I write but to myself and me
> What God's good grace doth in my soul imprint:
> I bought it not for pelf, none buys of thee
> Nor will I let it at so base a rent
> > As wealth or fame, which is but dross and vapour
> > And scarce deserves the blotting of a paper.

Nor am I so affected unto rime
But as it is a help to memory
Because it doth command a larger time
To wrap up sense in measure's quantity.
    Nor mars its truth, but gives wit's fire more fuel
    And from an ingot forms a curious jewel.

And though some amorous idiots do disgrace it
In making verse the packhorse of their passion
Such clouds may dim the sun but not deface it:
Nor marvel I that love doth love this fashion
    To speak in verse, if sweet and smoothly carried
    To true proportions love is ever married.

'Tis love hath wove this rugged twine of mine
Quickening my heart with such a sprightly flame
That frozen death can never make it pine
Nor sad affliction hath the power to lame
    For love and fire each other best resemble
    Both hot and bright, both vigilant and nimble.

Away base world, hence shadows, hence away.
You shall be no co-rivals to my love:
For he is fresh as is the flowery may
And truly constant as the turtle dove
    His breath like beds of roses cheer the morn
    His hair's reflex the sun-beams doth adorn.
                    (Southwell, 1997, pp. 131–52)

Note the care taken to justify her poetry and to disassociate it from popular verse. There is an insistence that her verse is a pursuit of truth – she is not in the business of 'smooth[ing] up vice with eloquent discourse'. Neither does she write for money or fame – her motives are pure, and the claim underlying the whole of this poem is that verse can speak of divinity – her experience of and reflections on God. She disclaims wealth and fame, claims the power of poetry as a mnemonic device and then, having scorned those poets who make verse 'the packhorse of their passion', goes on to sanctify the use of amorous imagery by applying it to her love of God in final stanzas which echo that most eroto-poetic portion of Scripture – the Song of Songs. In a poem of six stanzas, four are taken up with a justification of her use of poetry as an appropriate voice for divinity. Four in argument, that two may sing their deeply personal and proud declaration of her love for God.

Herbert, on the other hand (though he also struggled privately with the same accusatory voices, and struggled to find a way to write 'holy poetry'), is not always so apologetic in his verse. In his well-loved poem 'Prayer' he launches in boldly without explanation or introduction, certainly without apology. That prayer and poetry may go together, may inform and reform each other, is asserted in every line. This is no matter of mere adornment, of dressing his divinity in pretty phrases and soft tones. And there is no sense that he must justify anything; quite the reverse. The unspoken premise of this poem is more than the mere acceptability of the poetic register to voice theology; the unspoken premise is that poetry is not only an adequate form, but that it is the best form. The first word its only introduction, the rest exploration, connection, revelation. It could not have been done in prose.

Prayer [I]

Prayer, the church's banquet, angel's age,
    God's breath in man returning to his birth,
    The soul in paraphrase, heart in pilgrimage,
The Christian plummet sounding heaven and earth;
Engine against the Almighty, sinner's tower,
    Reversèd thunder, Christ-side-piercing spear,
    The six days' world-transposing in an hour,
A kind of tune, which all things hear and fear;
Softness, and peace, and joy, and love, and bliss,
    Exalted manna, gladness of the best,
    Heaven in ordinary, man well dressed,
The Milky Way, the bird of Paradise,
    Church bells beyond the stars heard, the soul's blood,
    The land of spices, something understood.

(Herbert, quoted in Witherspoon and Warnke (eds), 1963, p. 849)

This is one of the most famous and best loved poems on prayer and poetry that I know. At once concise and expansive. Bold and humble, lofty and meek, inclusive, human, this is more than definition, more than explanation. To read the poem, even in all its old familiarity, is to see again the marvellous height and depth and breadth of prayer, and to be drawn into the familiar made holy, and the holy made accessible.

And so, even in this age which was in many ways hostile to poetry as an expression of divinity, we see that the marriage of poetry and prayer could be fruitful. There is something about the two which is, despite what the plain-spoken truth-loving person (which may be any of us) might fear, essentially similar.

Look at some of the similarities. Both prayer and poetry concern themselves with making a connection between the inner world of spirit and imagination, and the outer world of sensory experience. 'I credit poetry,' writes Seamus Heaney in his 1995 Nobel Lecture, 'for making possible a fluid and restorative relationship between the mind's centre and its circumference' (Heaney, 1998, p. 450). Substitute 'soul' for 'mind' in that statement and you would find yourself part of a long continuum of religious writers whose concern it has been to explore the capacities of the soul. Could it be that prayer makes possible a fluid and restorative relationship between the soul's centre and its circumference? And could this restorative relationship be, in fact, redemption?

Forging this link between centre and circumference, between interior and exterior relies on an interplay between word and silence. In prayer as well as in poetry, the force may be carried as much in the space between the words as in the words themselves. There is a sense of waiting, of expectancy, which neither prayer nor poetry can do without. And there is quiet. There is pace, and timing and an appreciation of rhythms. Regular rhythms of prayer have been at the heart of the Christian monastic traditions for centuries; rhythms of the regular offices themselves, and, within each office, rhythms of voice and ear, antiphonal responses and corporate attentiveness.

All that I have said so far about interior and exterior and about rhythm and silence in poetry and prayer could be applied either to public or private prayer. And so far I have made no distinction between the two. But it is primarily to public prayer that I now want to turn our attention, to our liturgies (of whatever denomination) however loosely or carefully constructed. They are where the largest bodies of practising Christians meet week by week, they are the vehicles of our corporate speech, the mouth of our rites and a face we show to the world. In the language of our liturgies our thoughts about God are formed and reformed. And reformation of liturgy is a business about which the Church of England is particularly concerned now at the beginning of a new millennium.

In all of this there is a concern for truth. And here is where we come back to our beginning in the seventeenth century; with one very significant difference. Whereas in the seventeenth century the fear we have noted was that rime might mar truth, our modern problem is that there is, in the world around us, no common profession of the existence of universal or objective truth out there somewhere which might be marred. The Church may claim such truth, but she is a lone voice. Science is fact; poetry is fancy. Truth is, at best, elusive. And so, facing the anxiety of a faith which seems to have lost its relevance, encumbered as it is by its history of repression and oppression, and struggling to proclaim a living God in an age of agnosticism, and doctrinal certainty in a milieu of perhaps postmodern or perhaps relativistic individualism, we tremble. We are torn by the need to make the faith accessible and at the same time keep it from being so diluted and relativized that it ceases to have any unique significance. We fear a creed which has lost its bottom line.

Literalism and definition seem to be the obvious answers to both these problems of accessibility and certainty. Through clear and literal definition, our liturgies may be explained rather than obscured and our creeds kept from being eroded. For these very under-standable reasons we are drawn towards definition: define and defend. Get rid of obfuscatory and intellectually élitist language. In an age growing less literate and highly acclimatized to the swift changing image of screen and the one-second sound-bite, there is less room in our liturgies for the laborious though beautiful arcane intricacies of poetry. It is one luxury we just cannot afford right now.

Neither Puritan tracts nor the whim of a king dictate that it should be so, but the contemporary religious thinker who would use poetic language may find resonances here with the divine poets of the seventeenth century who found themselves in postures of defence.

And yet these two concerns of accessibility and certainty are real and need to be addressed. What we are talking about is no less than redemption, the 'need and chance/to salvage everything, to re-envisage/the zenith and glimpsed jewels of any gift/mistakenly abased' ('Station Island' in Heaney, 1998, pp. 242–68). There is a Christian imperative to speak and to speak in a way that will be understood.

It is for these very reasons that the poetic has been chosen again and again, by the mystics and the prophets and the wisdom writers. Not because it defines, precisely because it does not. Because it speaks directly to the heart, at the same time allowing room for the Spirit of God to inspire further. This is where poetic language becomes dangerous – in its continued openness to interpretation. Let us not pretend that poetry is safe. Metaphor is mistrustworthy. There is a power in imaginative language that perhaps ought to be feared: where it can take you, how far it will go. And that is part of its effectiveness.

The other part of its effectiveness is its rooting in the past. Our individual and our corporate pasts. Poetic language, when it works, works because it connects with something we have known. It is both signpost and reminder.

In his Nobel lecture, Seamus Heaney tells the story he heard as a boy of St Kevin who, whilst he was kneeling in prayer with his arms outstretched in the shape of the cross, became the unlikely roosting place for a blackbird. The blackbird mistook his hand for a kind of branch and swooped down and laid her clutch of eggs and began to nest. Heaney writes: 'Kevin stayed immobile for hours and days and nights and weeks, holding out his hand until the eggs hatched and the fledglings grew wings, true to life if subversive of common sense, at the intersection of natural process and the glimpsed ideal, at one and the same time a signpost and a reminder.' Heaney says that St Kevin was 'manifesting that order of poetry which is true to all that is appetitive in the intelligence and prehensile in the affections. An order where we can at last grow up to that which we stored up as we grew' (Heaney, 1998, p. 459). It seems to me that there is much in what he says of poetry that could be applied to prayer. Kevin's act made Kevin's life both a kind of prayer and a kind of poem. So too, our public prayers need to stand 'at the intersection of natural process and the glimpsed ideal' to be at once signposts and reminders, drawing on both the appetite of the intellect and the primitive knowledge of the heart. Our liturgies need to be places where we can 'at last grow up to that which we stored up as we grew'.

It is in this way that the elements of poetry such as metaphor and symbol can, in fact, be more accessible than prosaic explanations. Where the explanation reduces by definition, 'not this, but this', ever closing in to a more specific and exact point, the whole effort of symbol is outward and expansive, 'it means this, yes, and this also, and yes, this too', as in the Paschal mysteries of light, water, fire, and the like. These are the basic stuff of poetry.

In fact, we use metaphor all the time in our prayers. 'Give us this day our daily bread', 'The Lord is my shepherd', 'I am the vine, you are the branches', 'For thine is the kingdom'. These are the phrases we remember, the phrases that re-member us, the phrases we love and repeat in our dying when all other memory is gone. There is a wonderful inclusivity in metaphor, which allows people to bring their experience to bear on the meaning of a word or phrase. Perhaps that is why we love them. The metaphors mean something particular to us. Yes, we know the daily bread means all our daily, physical needs; but for you that smells of mother's kitchen and for me it may taste of rye. And we are each allowed to carry that with us into the corporate prayer. Wherever we are, whatever we bring, metaphor is a wider door than definition.

There is a newness too to metaphor, which works in much the same way as its inclusivity. A metaphorical phrase or image becomes new with the new experiences of life which we bring to it. And when we exchange images, as it were, each telling the other what reading of the metaphor we carry, the whole image expands. So also, when we learn what meanings may have been carried to that metaphor by those who preceded us, our appreciation grows. So the daily bread of manna was not the same as the unleavened bread of the Passover which is not the same as our sliced Hovis or our fresh out of the bread-maker crusty white. And yet it is. And so the metaphor lives in a way that mere explanation does not, at once referring us back and pointing us forward; a signpost and a reminder.

The metaphor is a signpost at a turning-point, where a decision is to be made, where a change can happen. There was a choice St Kevin made, a choice so small that it was hardly worth recording. Heaney has made a poem out of it (or you might say the choice was already a poem which he transcribed).

St Kevin and the Blackbird

And then there was St Kevin and the blackbird.
The saint is kneeling, arms stretched out, inside
His cell, but the cell is narrow, so

One turned-up palm is out the window, stiff
As a crossbeam, when a blackbird lands
And lays in it and settles down to nest.

Kevin feels the warm eggs, the small breast, the tucked
Neat head and claws and, finding himself linked
Into the network of eternal life,

Is moved to pity: now he must hold his hand
Like a branch out in the sun and rain for weeks
Until the young are hatched and fledged and flown.
                              *
And since the whole thing's imagined anyhow,
Imagine being Kevin. Which is he?
Self-forgetful or in agony all the time

From the neck on out down through his hurting forearms?
Are his fingers sleeping? Does he still feel his knees?
Or has the shut-eyed blank of underearth

Crept up through him? Is there distance in his head?
Alone and mirrored clear in love's deep river,
'To labour and not to seek reward,' he prays,

A prayer his body makes entirely
For he has forgotten self, forgotten bird
And on the riverbank forgotten the river's name.

                    (Heaney, 1998, pp. 410–11)

'A prayer his body makes entirely'. It seems to me that what we have described here is a fusion of prayer and poetry with the self so that the three are seamlessly woven, self, poetry and prayer. He lives the poem and the prayer. That is the rare life of a saint. But there are other ways of beginning to make those connections. 'Read poems as prayers', writes Heaney ('Station Island' in Heaney, 1998, pp. 242–68). Perhaps we could read prayers as poems, as well.

This is not because poetry is more beautiful, but for the same reasons the divine poets of the seventeenth century argued in defence of the poetic register: it is scriptural, memorable and simple. Light, fire, water, bread, wine. We have before us every day the symbols of Christian faith and the stuff of poetry. Let the Church speak its faith, then, in prayers that matter.* For what we are really looking for in our language of prayer is transformation. Making possible the hope of redemption in the here and now, in the mundane, and everyday, where our lapses are. Seeing in the small action the possibility of a transfigured moment. Listening to calls of glory, recognizing annunciations. Our public prayer needs to give congregations and individual persons the vehicles of revelation. I would suggest that prayers infused with poetry have the most power to do this. Heaney credits poetry with having 'the power to persuade that vulnerable part of our consciousness of its rightness in spite of the evidence of wrongness all around it, the power to remind us that we are hunters and gatherers of values, that our very solitudes and distresses are creditable, in so far as they, too, are an earnest of our veritable human being' (Heaney, 1998, p. 467). Being truly human, not being esoteric or aesthetic or élitist, that is what poetry has always been about. Let us not shadow the seventeenth-century notion of poetry as the enemy of truth, neither let us fall prey to the error of our age which confuses the words 'evidence' and 'truth'. Literal meanings have their place. But let our prayers be transformations of the literal, places where the familiar is made holy and the holy made accessible. Heaney tells how for him, Keats' 'Ode to Autumn' was 'an ark of the covenant between language and sensation' (Heaney, 1998, p. 450). May our prayers stand like that, at once local and eternal, exploring

---

*i.e. that have matter or substance; this is not to say that unpoetic prayers somehow do not 'count.'

the centre and circumference of the soul so that when the 'amen' echoes, there may be, in the silence, a sense that we have been to a place where we may say: '(now the ears of my ears awake and/now the eyes of my eyes are opened)' (cummings, 1959, p. 114).

References

Clarke, E., *Theory and Theology in the Work of George Herbert*. Clarendon Press, Oxford, 1997.

cummings, e. e., *100 Selected Poems*. Grove Press, New York, 1959.

de Saluste, G., *The Divine Weeks and Works*, tr. J. Sylvester, ed. S. Snyder. Clarendon Press, Oxford, 1979.

Doelman, J., 'The Accession of King James I and English Religious Poetry', *Studies in English Literature* 34 (1994), pp. 19–40.

Hall, J., *The Collected Poems of Joseph Hall*, ed. A. Davenport. Liverpool University Press, Liverpool, 1949.

Heaney, S., *Opened Ground: Selected Poems, 1966–1996*. Faber & Faber, London, 1998.

Southwell, Lady Anne, 'Precept 4', in *The Southwell-Sibthorpe Commonplace Book*, ed. J. Klene. Medieval and Renaissance Texts and Studies, Tempe, Arizona, 1997, pp. 151–2.

Witherspoon, A., and Warnke, F. (eds), *Seventeenth-Century Prose and Poetry*, 2nd edn. Harcourt, Brace and World, New York, 1963.

Further Reading

Allchin, A. M., *The World is a Wedding*. Darton, Longman & Todd, London, 1978.

Brown, D. and Fuller, D. *Signs of Grace: Sacraments in Poetry and Prose*. Cassell, London, 1995.

Dillard, A., *Teaching a Stone to Talk*. Picador, London, 1984.

Ecclestone, A., *Yes to God*. Darton, Longman & Todd, London, 1975.

Ecclestone, A., *A Staircase for Silence*. Darton, Longman & Todd, London, 1977.

Hammarskjöld, D., *Markings*. Faber & Faber, London, 1964.

Mayne, M., *This Sunrise of Wonder*. HarperCollins, London, 1995.

Traherne, T., *Centuries*. Clarendon Press, Oxford, 1960.

CHAPTER SIX

Prayer and Music

Jeremy Begbie

When people pray, the urge to make music seems almost irresistible. In virtually every religious tradition, when a god is addressed in prayer, music is not far away. Christianity is no exception. From the first stirrings of the Church, prayer was often wedded to song – we see traces of that in the New Testament, where passages can take on a hymn-like structure (e.g. 1 Timothy 3.16). And since New Testament times, the impulse to voice melodies, pluck or strike strings and blow air through tubes has often gone hand in hand with prayer. We need only think of the centuries of plainsong, the monumental choral prayers of Bach, the 'singing in tongues' of Pentecostal praise, the searing liturgical symphonies of James MacMillan, the rave music of 'alternative worship', the sung prayers of the Orthodox liturgy. To be sure, there have been times when the Church has been suspicious of music, even disdainful, but for most of Christian history, prayer and music have been close allies.

Along with this, the language of prayer and 'spirituality' is often applied to the experience of music, even by those who have nothing to do with the Church or any specific religion. The band 'Faithless' sing of a 'rave' club-night in these words: 'This is my church. This is where I heal my hurt. For tonight, God is a DJ.' Pick a music magazine off the shelves of a newsagent and it is not hard to find phrases like 'a spiritual performance', 'transcendent sound', 'a sacred moment'.

Despite all this, it is quite rare to find anyone asking, '*Why* has music been linked to prayer so frequently?' Or, to put it another way, '*What is it that music contributes to prayer?*' The question is in fact a very large one. Music can perform many different functions and can accompany prayer in very diverse ways. Further, there are many different ways of praying. With limited space, we can only consider a few features of music and a few forms of prayer. Nonetheless, we can throw at least some light on why music has been so persistent a partner of prayer, and, in the process, I hope, be given a deeper understanding of the nature of prayer itself.

A Little Clarity

Two cautionary points need to be made before we begin. First, *a little clarity goes a long way*. Take the word 'music'. Anthropologists of music are fond of saying that there is no such thing as music, only 'musics', and these vary greatly. To pretend that, say, Javanese Gamelan can be put in the same category as the band 'Blur' risks doing violence to both. We need to be clear, then, about what we might mean when we speak of 'music'. In this chapter we are concentrating on 'Western tonal music', which came to fruition towards the end of the seventeenth century in Europe and has come to pervade Western culture. It is ordered according to a central note around which are situated other notes of lesser importance. It operates largely through patterns of tension and resolution. Tonal music encompasses not only a vast amount of so-called 'classical' music, but almost all Western 'popular' music. It is the music of REM and Rachmaninov, Sibelius and the Spice Girls. It is the kind of music the readers of this book will probably know best, and that is why I am limiting myself to it. (This is not to say that it is necessarily better or more valuable than other kinds of music, nor that it is the only music which can enrich prayer.)

Then there is the word 'prayer' and its slithery companion, 'spirituality'. Here also, a little clarity goes a long way. I take Christian prayer to be conversation with the God who has declared himself supremely and decisively in Jesus Christ – in short the God of the Scriptures who is Father, Son and Spirit. It is, I believe, important to say this. The language of prayer and spirituality is often enthusiastically applied to certain types of music, when it is not at all obvious that the language is being used in any distinctively Christian way. While this may be quite harmless in some contexts, and may well tell us something important about our society's quest for the transcendent, if we want to trace the links between music and a particular tradition of prayer, we need some clarity about which God (if any) might be the object of the prayer we are considering. Otherwise, we open ourselves to confusion, and might well do both the music and the prayer an injustice.

Two examples will help illustrate this. An album was recently released entitled 'The Prayer Cycle', described on the cover notes as 'a multi-lingual choral symphony aimed at exploring the nature of spiritual supplication'. Among others, it featured Alanis Morissette, James Taylor and John Williams. Judging by the music, it seems that 'spiritual supplication' must be serene, meditative and extremely beautiful. In some respects (though not all), the music resembles that of John Tavener, who since his conversion to Orthodoxy has been hugely popular not just in so-called 'classical' circles, but much further afield. His music is often hailed as 'prayerful' and profoundly 'spiritual'. Without for a moment denying that 'The Prayer Cycle' and Tavener's music may indeed enable some people to pray more deeply and may be tapping into a widespread yearning for God, we need to ask some pointed questions when it is supposed that this kind of music takes us to the core of what it is to be prayerful or spiritual. Why assume that spiritual music has to be slow? Why assume that being close to God necessarily means suppressing change and movement? Why assume that prayerful music has to be rhythmically muted, with a minimum of contrast and a uniform texture? Why assume that simplicity is necessarily more spiritual or prayerful than complexity? Why assume that true spirituality is marked by the evasion of conflict and tension? Even a glance at the pages of the Bible will challenge all of these assumptions. Prayer comes in many different forms – for instance, it can be angry and raging as well as relaxed and receptive. In the writings of the Apostle Paul, to be 'spiritual' means to be animated by the Holy Spirit, and life in the Spirit can include periods of acute opposition and suffering as well as gentle assurance and rest.

This is not to deny that music which is relatively slow, quiet and homogenous may be especially helpful for some types of prayer. But if it is the Christian God we have in mind, we should be careful not to allow such music to dominate our view of what it is to be prayerful or spiritual. Music suitable for prayer can include a wide variety of options.

Music Interacts in Its Own Ways

A second word of caution. It is easy to think about music as if it came 'on its own'. I am sometimes asked about a piece of music, 'Is it harmful?' I always have to answer, 'A lot depends on what comes with it.' Music always comes with a context, and the context affects what we hear, sometimes quite radically. At a U2 concert, we hear the music along with images on a giant screen; at a string quartet performance, we hear the music along with the gestures of the players. What we receive from music depends to a large extent on the way it engages with these other factors. Many concert audiences will squirm during Alban Berg's *Chamber Concerto* in the Carnegie Hall; but they will not ask for their money back when the same kind of music accompanies *film noir*. When Pavarotti sings Puccini's 'Nessun Dorma' in an opera house, the notes are used by a Prince singing of his beloved; on TV the same notes can introduce coverage of the World Cup; in Starbucks, it performs a different function again. And, of course, there is an extensive range of cultural factors which affect the way we hear music – upbringing, conventions, education, and so on. 'Music alone' is a fiction. Instead of asking, 'Is this music harmful?', we ought to be asking, '*What is the music doing in this context*, in this building, with these people, with these images, etc.?'

Does this mean context is everything? Can any pattern of notes 'mean' anything? No. Certain patterns of notes lend themselves readily to some uses more than others. For example, one of the commonest forms of music worldwide is the lullaby – lullabies generally have smooth descending melodic lines, they are usually slow with a relatively simple structure and much repetition. You would not use lullabies to call people to battle. Patterns of notes, that is, have their own properties and human beings are physiologically and psychologically 'wired' in some ways and not others – this means that although there can be a wide range of responses to any given piece of music, it will not be an unlimited range.

Nevertheless, having said this, what we receive from music will depend to a large extent on its interaction with its context. It is especially important to remember this if we set the words of prayers to music. Typically, when music and words are combined, there have

70

been two main ways of understanding the relation between them, lying at two ends of a spectrum of possibilities. On the one hand, it is thought, music can *contest* words (or vice versa). So, for example, music can 'get in the way' of words – when an organist over-elaborates the harmony in the last verse of a hymn, or when words get lumbered with a melody which is wholly inappropriate. On the other hand, it is thought, music can *conform* to words. Sometimes it is just assumed that this will happen: if we get the words right, the music will just buckle down and fall into place. Significantly, a great deal of writing about music in worship is about the words that are sung, not the music, the assumption being that the music will take care of itself as long as the words are acceptable. Sometimes, when people realize this is simply naive (for music has enormous power in its own right), they will go to great pains to ensure that the music does conform as strictly as possible to the words. The Reformer John Calvin, for example, was very eager to ensure that the Psalms were set to music which matched the words in every possible respect.

However, to see the possible relations between music and words running along a line from 'contesting' to 'conforming' is inadequate. For this is to forget that music *interacts* and in *its own ways.* When we sing a prayer like 'Lord, have mercy' to an African American spiritual tune, the music (among other things) brings out emotional depths in the words, and the words in turn affect the way we hear the music; they interact with each other to create a highly potent effect. Moreover, music never simply apes or mimics words; it contributes something of its own. It interacts in its own ways. Otherwise, we would never bother to set any words to music!

This brings us back to our main question: just what is it that music can give to prayer? What are its special features? Here I have space only to speak about three of them.

Sound Mix

One of the most obvious features of Western music of the last few hundred years is that it includes notes which sound simultaneously. Unremarkable as this may seem, it is a fact with far-reaching implications.

Consider the world we see. A painter knows that you cannot have red and yellow on a canvas in the same space, and have them visible *as* red and yellow. What happens? One colour hides the other, or (if the paint is wet) they merge into some kind of orange. And, clearly, you cannot have the same patch of colour in two places at the same time.

Obvious as all this may seem to the eye, it is not obvious to the ear. If I play a note on the piano – say, middle C – the note fills the whole of my heard 'space'. I cannot identify some zone where the note is and somewhere it is not. I cannot say, 'It is here, but not there.' Unlike the patch of red on a canvas, it is, in a sense, everywhere. Of course, I can identify the source of the note (the vibrating string), and its location ('It is over there'). But what I *hear* does not occupy a bounded area. It fills the entirety of my aural space.

If I play a second note – say, the E above middle C – along with middle C, that second note also fills the whole of my heard space. Yet I hear it as a distinct note. The notes interpenetrate; they occupy the same 'space' but I can hear them as two notes. Notes like this neither hide each other, nor merge. (Of course, I can play one note so loud that the other is not heard; but the point here is that it is possible to hear them as distinct in the same heard space.)

Music exploits this feature of sound perception. Through its dynamic combinations of simultaneously sounding notes, it gives us an experience of a special kind of togetherness, where things do not obscure each other or merge, but interpenetrate while being perceived as distinct.

If I add a third note to my two-note chord, it is hard not to think of the Trinity. Arguably, many of the Church's problems with the Trinity have arisen because we have too quickly assumed that God must be, if not visible, at least amenable to the way our visual perception works. So, typically, we are left with two extremes: tritheism (three gods), or unitarianism (one God without any distinctions). These are the two basic possibilities you can visualize. (There are, of course, some subtle options in between, and some wonderful visual representations of the Trinity. And the world of sound has its own drawbacks when it comes to evoking the Trinity. But the main point here still stands: there is a particular limitation with visual representations of the Trinity which does not hold in the case of sound.) Quite how the Father and the Son can be 'in' each other (as in John's Gospel), and the Spirit 'in' both!, is notoriously hard to visualize, but it is akin to the common experience of anyone who hears three notes together. We cannot *see* threeness and oneness in the same space clearly, but we can *hear* them both without difficulty.

We can take this a step further. A three-note chord on a piano can 'set off' certain other strings (if they are left free to vibrate), without those other strings being struck. The strings start to vibrate in sympathy because they get caught up in the resonance of the three-note chord; they are freed to vibrate in their own way.

What has this to do with prayer? Prayer in the Christian tradition is trinitarian through and through. As the New Testament makes evident, when we pray, we do not fire arrows optimistically at a singular, disengaged God, far from us. We are caught up in the divine resonance of Father, Son and Spirit. Romans 8 makes the pattern wonderfully clear. We do not know what to pray for or how to pray, but the Spirit intercedes in us and for us (8.26), the Spirit who is in tune with the will of God (8.27). The Spirit enables us to belong to Christ (8.9–11), and releases the cry 'Abba! Father!' (8.15–16). Our prayer, therefore, can resonate with Christ, who himself prays for us (8.34). Prayer is something which happens within us and around us. When we get drawn into this divine movement, we will not be smothered by God, nor will we be merged so that we lose our identity. Like those other strings which are freed to vibrate in their own way, we will become more fully ourselves, more human. Of course, I am not claiming that music will suddenly make all this magically happen, but music does have particular powers which make it especially apt to help us become part of this extraordinary trinitarian momentum of prayer.

Now let us expand this further. Jesus prays that his disciples would be one, as he and his Father are one (John 17.11). The love which binds them together is to be that 'interpenetrating' love which binds Father and Son. Bearing in mind all we have been saying about togetherness and distinctiveness through overlapping sounds, it is perhaps not surprising that singing together in harmony has been so prevalent in the Christian tradition. During a recent visit to South Africa, a number of times I sang the national anthem, 'Nkosi Sikelel' iAfrika' – a prayer to God. It evoked in me an extraordinary sense of togetherness, even though I hardly knew the hymn and often hardly knew the people with whom I was singing. Part of the reason for that was that I knew this song had held thousands together during the fierce decades of *apartheid*. Part of it was the overwhelming welcome I received at most of the assemblies where I sang the hymn. But a large part of it was also its four-part harmony, in which no vocal line predominates over the others (unlike the British national anthem!). In this kind of singing, your voice and all the others fill the same heard 'space'. It is a space not of many voices each with their mutually exclusive and bounded 'place', but a space of overlapping sounds, an uncrowded space without 'edges' where distinct voices mutually establish each other. Why was solidarity in South Africa so often expressed in harmonious song during the years of oppression? Among the many reasons, I suggest, is that when crowds met to sing – in camps, townships, churches, marches – the *music* provided a taste of authentic freedom, when in virtually every other sense they were *not* free. Why is it that prayers for freedom and reconciliation have so often been sung in this way? Because, I suggest, people are being given a taste – in sound – of the concord for which they are praying and which the trinitarian gospel makes possible.

Tensions and Resolutions

A second very basic feature of Western tonal music is that it generally operates through patterns of tension and resolution. These come in many different forms. One of them is harmonic tension and resolution, when certain chords (such as the dominant seventh) are used to arouse a sense of incompleteness and anticipation, this tension being resolved by more stable chords. Resolution can come very quickly, or after a long period. A common structure of songs is ABA – where a theme (A) is stated and perhaps repeated, followed by a move 'away' to very different material (B), often in a different key, followed by a 'return' of the main theme (A) (as in George Gershwin's 'I got rhythm'). B generates a tension which is resolved in the repeat of A.

Tensions and resolutions work concurrently at many different levels and over different time-scales. The most famous symphony

74

ever written, Beethoven's Fifth, is a good example – the titanic struggles of the first and third movements are resolved in the blazing C-major glory of the last; within the last movement, tensions between keys and themes are dissipated in the final bars; within even single bars, micro-tensions and resolutions push us ever forward. This kind of multi-levelled matrix gives Western music its characteristic 'forward-moving' feel. We want the tensions to resolve. We are made to expect and want more, hope for more.

It is not hard to trace the connections between this and the Christian faith. What Christians call 'salvation' is God's giant resolution process, arising from the tension caused by human sin and evil, reaching completion in the new heaven and earth (Revelation 21). At the heart of this lies the crucifixion and resurrection of Christ, *the* central climactic tension and resolution. And to live in Christ by the Spirit, as the New Testament constantly reminds us, brings a whole series of tensions and resolutions – pushing us forward in hope, some of the tensions being brought about by our own sinfulness, others by the opposition and resistance which the Christian life necessarily entails.

Music's tensions and resolutions not only help us to understand more deeply these movements of tension and resolution in God's purposes, they can also serve to embody or enact them. This, surely, is one of the reasons why music is so well suited to being associated with prayer, for prayer – if it is conversation with the Christian God – is bound to get caught up in the multi-levelled tensions and resolutions of salvation.

In dialogue with music, let us draw out just one implication of this. Music, of course, takes time to happen, and because it does, it schools us in the art of *patience*. Certainly, we can play or sing a piece faster, but this is possible only to a very limited degree before it becomes incoherent. Also, we can 'cut and paste' music today in ways unimaginable to our forebears: we can hop from track to track on the CD, flip from one rock number to another, buy highlights of a three-hour opera. But few would claim they hear a work in its integrity by doing this. Music says to us, 'There are some things you will learn only by going through this process, by being taken into this succession of notes.' There is a direct link with prayer here, especially with contemplative prayer. As Rowan Williams puts it:

if music is the most fundamentally contemplative of the arts, it is *not* because it takes us into the timeless but because it obliges us to rethink time: it is no longer time for action, achievement, dominion and power, not even time for acquiring ideas...It is simply time for feeding upon reality; quite precisely like that patient openness to God that is religious contemplation.

As such, music can be a moral event, for it 'tells us what we are and what we are not, creatures, not gods, creators only when we remember that we are not the Creator, and so are able to manage the labour and attention and expectancy that belongs to art' (Williams, 1994, pp. 248-9).

But there is a kind of patience which is particularly hard to learn, and which the writers of the Bible often address – patience in the midst of delay, when the resolution does not come as expected. Very common in the Bible is a sense that God has in some way 'held back' the fulfilment of his promises – the deliverance of Israel from Egypt, the end of Israel's exile, the coming of the Holy Spirit, the end of human history. Indeed, this sense of delay and the patience that needs to be learned in the midst of it seems intrinsic to Christian faith: 'if we hope for what we do not see, we wait for it with patience' (Romans 8.25). Music can be very instructive here. One of the key skills in composing is negotiating the 'dynamic space' between a tension and its subsequent resolution. A great deal of musicology has studied the very common technique of 'deferred gratification', holding up a resolution through diversions, digressions and pauses. A simple example can be found in that piece learned by every beginner and encased in a million telephone answering machines – 'Für Elise' by Beethoven. On the first page, the composer inserts an extra bar just before the main melody returns – gratification is deferred, with the result that we are 'pulled in' to the piece more strongly. Much more sophisticated is the second movement of Brahms' Second Symphony where only at the very end of the piece are we given the key chord unambiguously on a strong beat: Brahms makes us wait until the last bar.

Interestingly, common as this device is in the Western repertoire, in contemporary music for worship – including settings of prayers – it is remarkably rare. In most hymnbooks and song books today, musical goals are reached with a deadening predictability, with little sense that fulfilment might be something which has to be waited for patiently. Could it be that what theologians have often spotted in some circles in the Church – a craving for immediate gratification, a loss of the 'not yet' dimension of Christian life – is finding its counterpart in the music? Perhaps the greatest service we can offer to church musicians is to encourage them to explore and compose types of music that are not presumptuous, that give voice to the truth that instant results are not of the essence of faith, that our hope is not yet realized in all its fullness, that prayer involves patient waiting.

The waiting, of course, need not be empty. It is a repeated motif in Scripture that, although delay can be frustrating, mysterious and sometimes can appear simply as unjust ('How long O Lord?'), it can also be a means through which our trust in God is strengthened, and through which we are 'pulled in' to God's purposes more deeply. In the New Testament, patience is often associated with growth in steadfastness and faith through perseverance in the midst of opposition (see, for example, Hebrews 11). Music can offer much here, for it can introduce us to a 'meantime' where there is an acute sense of delay but which is at the same time enormously enriching.

Music does this most powerfully through silence. All composers and musicians know that silence is one of the most effective tools they have. The opening of the theme music of the film *Jaws* generates its 'edge-of-the-seat' terror largely through silence. The final bars of Sibelius' Fifth Symphony are, in essence, silence punctuated by six chords, creating an extraordinarily intense longing for resolution. In this example, the silences become highly charged because of the memory of what has been and the anticipation of what will be; so we are 'pulled' more profoundly into the music's drama. One of the hardest aspects of the Christian life is handling the silences of God, the apparently dead 'in between' times. Music can remind us of the power of memory and anticipation – the memory of what God has done in Jesus Christ, and in that, the promise of what he will finally do for the world. This can draw us back into God's ways with the world, and thus renew our trust and hope. Something of this dynamic, surely, needs to find its way into at least some forms of silent prayer. Music does more than help us understand the dynamic. It enacts it for us, it offers the experience of a potentially empty silence becoming full, vibrant and charged with hope. The conjunction of prayer with music which includes silence has a great deal to offer.

Purified Prayer

A third feature of much music, which can also add much to our experience and understanding of prayer, is what we might call its 'representative' role. To put it simply, great music often 'says' what we *would* 'say' if we could. Consider, for example, music's emotional power, about which so much has been written. Some speak about music mirroring our emotions, some about music resembling our emotions, some about music giving vent to our emotions, and so on. While there is truth in all of these, I believe that more central to music's emotional power is its ability to *purify* and concentrate our emotional life. In day-to-day living our emotions are often confused and transient – they are cloudy; they 'jump out' at us unexpectedly; they are caught up in tangles of desires; some are overt, some hidden; and they are often wildly out of control. Music at its best does more than 'express' emotion, it offers us, in sound, patterns of intensified, purified emotion – as when J. S. Bach evokes the joy of heavenly song in the 'Sanctus' of his Mass in B minor, or when a Scottish piper winds a poignant lament over a windswept graveside. The musician, as it were, takes our muddled and confused feelings, refines and concentrates them in sound, returning them to us with a new intensity and vitality. If our response could be put into words, it might well be something like, 'Yes, that's it . . . '

This representative role could be applied to many aspects of music. But the links with prayer are already not hard to see. One of the distinguishing marks of Christian prayer which we have mentioned in passing is that at its heart it involves one who himself prays on our behalf, Jesus Christ. All too often in the Western Church, Christ has become merely the daunting example of prayer, or merely the one to whom we direct our prayers. But the New Testament also speaks of Christ's active, continuing prayer for us. In the epistle to the Hebrews, Christ is the High Priest, tempted yet without sin, sympathizing with our weaknesses, unashamed to call us his brothers and sisters, and alive to intercede for us, appearing in God's presence on our behalf. Just as an ambassador on a foreign trip carries the needs of his or her country with them, focusing their people's concerns and speaking as they would speak if they could, so Christ takes our feeble, muddled and uncontrolled prayers, interprets and purifies them in the presence of 'Abba', Father. We are touching on a huge mystery here, but one of immense power and significance. We do not have to 'get it right' in order to be heard by God – we can, as it were, lean on Christ, knowing that he can bear up our cries before the Father more truly and authentically than we ever could ourselves. As we rely on the prayer of Christ in this way, we discover what it is we really desire, truly feel. Our own prayer is thus purged, reshaped and renewed, because now we see everything with and 'through Christ our Lord'. If we were to express it in words, we might come close to saying something like, 'Yes, that's it; that's what I want to say...'. In music, I am suggesting, a very similar momentum is at work, and moreover, that in the context of prayer, music can be used by Christ in just this way.

I have tried to point to just three features of music which lend themselves very readily to Christian prayer. We could carry on this enquiry much further. If we did, we would find not only many clues as to why the marriage between prayer and music has been so close, but that something of the very character of prayer is opened up for us afresh. Music has more to contribute to prayer than we might first imagine.

References

Williams, R., *Open to Judgement: Sermons and Addresses*. Darton, Longman & Todd, London, 1994.

Further Reading

Begbie, J. S., *Music in God's Purposes*. Handsel Press, Edinburgh, 1989.

Begbie, J. S., *Theology, Music and Time*. Cambridge University Press, Cambridge, 2000.

Campling, C. R., *The Food of Love: Reflections on Music and Faith.* SCM Press, London, 1997.

Cook, N., *Music: A Very Short Introduction.* Oxford University Press, Oxford, 1998.

Edgar, W., *Taking Note of Music.* SPCK, Third Way Books, London, 1986.

Frith, S., *Performing Rites: On the Value of Popular Music.* Oxford University Press, Oxford, 1996.

CHAPTER SEVEN

Prayer and Sexuality

Angela Tilby

Sexuality and Prayer: Definitions

What a fuss we Christians make about sexuality! I take sexuality to mean the nature of our drive towards emotional and physical union with other human beings. It is about identity, that is, our maleness or femaleness, for these are the two packages human beings come in. It is also about orientation, that is, what kind of others evoke an erotic interest in us. Seen like this, sexuality is a much wider and more fundamental aspect of our lives than simply 'having sex'. And prayer I take to be the expression of another fundamental drive, the drive towards spiritual union with the divine. Prayer in this sense is much wider than simply 'saying prayers'; it is about what is encompassed by the word 'spirituality', which would include our lifestyle, our beliefs about God, and the spiritual, physical, mental and emotional disciplines that enable us to be praying people. Both prayer and sexuality invite us to ways of knowing and being known which affect us very deeply.

A Conflict of Interest

Within the Christian matrix there does often seem to be a fundamental conflict of interest between sexuality and prayer. The conflict is succinctly expressed by G. A. Studdert Kennedy, 'Woodbine Willie' as he was known, the most famous army padre to have served in the First World War. His poem 'Temptation' from *The Unutterable Beauty*:

> Pray! Have I prayed! When I'm worn out with my praying!
> When I've bored the blessed angels with my battery of prayer!

It's the proper thing to say – but it's only saying, saying,
And I cannot get to Jesus for the glory of her hair.

(Studdert Kennedy, 1983, p. 24)

'With my body I thee worship,' bride says to groom and groom to bride in the marriage service in *The Book of Common Prayer*. This can cause consternation to pious couples who also know that there is only one legitimate object of worship, God. As the hymn puts it:

> The dearest idol I have known
> Whate'er that idol be
> Help me to tear it from thy throne
> And worship *only thee*.

Christianity is watchful lest sex becomes idolatry. The founder of analytical psychology, Carl Gustav Jung, son of a Lutheran pastor, had a numinous dream of the underworld in which he saw an erect phallus enthroned. Such a dream might express a legitimate fear of disordered sexuality, or simply the extent to which sexual power is driven underground in the Christian imagination. But fear and ignorance of sexuality, as much as excessive interest in it, can bring the self to shipwreck. Think of the peculiar sexual and emotional adventures of that group of lay Christian scholars who were prominent for their efforts in the re-moralization of Britain after the Second World War: C. S. Lewis, Charles Williams, J. R. R. Tolkien, Dorothy L. Sayers. However convincing their attempts at popular apologetic, their understanding of themselves as sexual and emotional beings seems to have been adrift from the rest of their lives. Charles Williams, the novelist, was married, and yet he fell deeply in love with another woman, and spent a great deal of emotional energy convincing himself of the splendours of Platonic love.

C. S. Lewis's story is well known. He seemed to his circle of friends to be extraordinarily blind to his own motives when he offered to go through a civil marriage to the American divorcee Joy Davidman in order to allow her to stay in this country. When he finally acknowledged his love for her he was appalled that the Church would not marry them because her first husband was still alive. He, like many others, discovered that sexual moral absolutes are fine until they affect you. Then one thinks of Dorothy L. Sayers, linguist and scholar and inventor of Lord Peter Wimsey. Her sex life was a disaster. First there was the heartless Russian lover, then the illegitimate child she hid from the world, and her eventual decision, born perhaps of weariness and resignation, to marry a car enthusiast – the only genuine interest they shared was booze. The only one of that group of famous Christians who seems to have been happily married was J. R. R. Tolkien and he spent his life fantasizing about hobbits.

What I see in these figures, and I see it in the lives of a surprising number of devout, praying Christians, is a curious lack of self-awareness and self-knowledge when it comes to issues of sexuality.

No Tidy Integration of Sexuality and Spirituality within the Christian Tradition

As I look at the structure of Christianity, particularly in its early forms, I find myself becoming aware that there are aspects of Christian spirituality that question and even actively undermine any easy or ideal integration of sexuality. There is the stark choice of lifestyle offered by Christian orthodoxy: marriage or celibacy, but Christian tradition and experience tell a more complicated story.

Other Faiths

By way of contrast, other faiths don't seem to have this difficulty. Consider Hindu religion. In temple worship the gods are depicted as creative and generative; the male and female are frequently intertwined. Male aspects of divinity have their female counterparts. There is Shiva and there is Shakti. Erotic language and imagery are freely used in devotion. The flirtation of the milkmaids with the god Krishna is a parable of the praying soul. Yet the pattern of Hindu domestic life assumes a fundamental distinction of role between the genders. There is almost no place for a single woman. Yet there is scope for a life of sexual renunciation, traditionally taken on by a husband and father when his family duties are over.

In Islam, God cannot be imaged in any way, and is far removed from gender. Yet human gender difference is sharply maintained.

Women need to be contained by men, and polygamy has the potential to soak up the spare women who need male protection. Marriage is normative and desirable; there is little scope for celibacy.

Christianity as Sexually Subversive

Both Hindus and Muslims appear to have no problems with sexuality and they tend to be extremely traditional when it comes to gender roles. The same could be said of Orthodox Jews. But Christianity has never been quite like that. The Gospels have a quietly subversive agenda when it comes to traditional expectations of sexual behaviour. One thinks of the virgin birth, the celibacy of Jesus, the violent eroticism of Herodias's daughter's dance which ends with the beheading of John the Baptist.

Christianity brings in a whiff of the exotic, the memory of a martyred Perpetua or a repentant Pelagia or an Origen (did he castrate himself?) or a tormented Augustine, or even an Etheldreda. Etheldreda was an illustrious Saxon queen who founded a Christian monastery at Ely. I preached recently on the feast of the translation of her incorrupt body. Married twice, she refused to have sex with her husbands and died a virgin. From lives like hers novel ways of living and praying are born which question the sexual assumptions of traditional societies. And these novel ways of living, flawed as they have sometimes been, often carry the mark of Christian authenticity.

So there is something within Christianity which makes the conjunction of prayer and sexuality untidy, difficult and perhaps potentially creative. I'd like now to try to trace a faint and inadequate outline of that untidiness from Paul to Augustine, in whose thought, I believe, we find a resource, if not for resolving the problem, at least for accepting that our partial solutions are worth persevering with.

St Paul and Sex: Teaching on Marriage and Prayer in the Light of Apocalyptic Expectation

St Paul gives advice on sex and marriage in 1 Corinthians 7. Paul is expecting the return of the Lord as the gospel spreads to the ends of the Gentile world. With his sense of apocalyptic urgency he is aware of the positive advantages of his own single state. To marry, in Paul's mind, is to take on a burden which the single are spared. I hear only a faint echo in Paul of the male puritanism of the Jewish sages; of Proverbs and Ecclesiasticus, where the assumption is that women are trouble on the whole and that you are exceptionally lucky, given the perversities of female nature, to find a good wife (and that means pure, quiet, competent, uncomplaining) who leaves you to get on with the things that really matter.

There is in Paul, by contrast, something new, a recognition of married people as spiritual and sexual equals in the Lord. It really is intriguing that Paul feels he has to tell married people not to deprive each other of sex. It's not quite where I would start with an engaged or married couple. He seems to think it is quite a good idea for married people to agree from time to time to abstain from sex in order to give themselves to prayer. But he warns them that they really ought to make sure that they recommence their sexual relationship once the time of intense prayer is over. He is worried that a Christian couple might become so absorbed in prayer that they put their marital relationship at risk, allowing the less spiritually ardent partner to be led astray.

The Jewish part of Paul accepts sex and marriage as a fact of life. They are part of what is given to mortals, along with work and leisure and food and drink. Marriage can be undertaken with a good conscience. But having said that we must also admit that, for Paul, sexuality doesn't contribute positively to spiritual growth. Hebrew and Jewish tradition knows of no heavenly consort; there is no Mrs Yahweh, and one of the things Jews find messy about paganism is the lure of the mysteries, the suspicion that what goes on in the dark of the pagan temple has sexual implications. Perhaps the Eleusinian mysteries did conclude with a sacramental epiphany, the secret worship of the mystery of generation in the form of an ear of corn.

When we read Paul today we often assume that he was a sexual puritan, full of hang-ups that contemporary believers now need to cast off. But that's because we read him as though his views were exceptional which, of course, they weren't. His assumptions about the place of sexuality were not at all odd for his time. Around him and in the make up of his Gentile converts was a sexual pessimism, which went far beyond his own teachings, and permeated the world in which Christianity was born. As the hope of the Lord's early return faded, this pessimism became more obvious and pervasive in Christian thinking.

The Sexual Pessimism of the Early Christian World

If it makes any sense to talk about where first-century people experienced themselves as selves, and perhaps we can only speak of a few educated, cultured males with enough material wealth and leisure to reflect on such things, the core of identity or 'selfhood' for such people was not in what we call sexuality, but in the mind.

Stoicism and the Tempering of Emotion

In the philosophy of Stoicism, Reason was the helmsman of the soul. Its task was to master the passions, to lift the self to that place of freedom which was described as *apatheia*, passionlessness or detachment. To live *kata logon*, according to reason, was serenity, peace, sanity, harmony with nature and with the divine reason which permeated all things. Stoicism had an enormous influence on early Christianity and its legacy lives on. It made it hard for devout Christians to manage the temporary psychosis of falling in love, or the possessiveness that arises in passionate relationships, or the heartbreak of loss, without the accompaniment of guilt and anxiety. On the other hand there is from the Stoic heritage another door opening up alongside that of Paul, towards a kind of equality between sexual partners in the simple dignity of quiet, mutual affection. Brutus's words to Portia in Shakespeare's *Julius Caesar* (Act II, scene 1) express this most movingly:

> You are my true and honourable wife
> as dear to me as are the ruddy drops
> that visit my sad heart.

The letters of that most abrasive early Christian apologist, Tertullian, to his wife have, surprisingly, something of that tenderness. The over-all impact of Stoic teaching was to encourage a distrust of strong feelings, a dampening of sexual enthusiasm, which, at the same time might well have enabled a particular quality of friendship between men and women.

Platonism: the Lure of the Monad

Platonism, on the other hand, exalts the cerebral and the celibate. The mission of the mind is to free itself from the distractions of the senses, lifting itself by ascetic practices and contemplation away from the material universe into the pure, cool beauty and unity of the intelligible world. In their encounter with Middle and Neo-Platonism the early Christians wrestled with the nature of the divine. If God is defined as ineffable, if to be God, God has to be beyond relationship, beyond movement, then the imitation of God must involve a one-way movement from the self to God, back to the source.

As to the divine mind itself, we must not underestimate the relentless monism of the ancient world. Stoic and Platonic philosophers taught not only that the divine was one, but uniquely and inviolably 'one and beyond the one'. Christians accepted this, of course, and assumed it *was* biblical monotheism, with only Clement of Alexandria suggesting that God might be not only beyond the One, but beyond Oneness itself. To the philosophers the multiplicity of the created world represented a fall from the divine simplicity, into time, variety, change and death. We are implicated in this simultaneous creation and fall. The ultimate spiritual task for human beings lies in finding the way back to the serene singularity of the one.

Giving up Sex to Find Oneself

How did these beliefs cash out in everyday life? Well, you might imagine a leisured Roman gentleman getting married and having children. Perhaps he has had passionate relationships with boys in his youth, perhaps he has a female slave who is also his concubine. He becomes reflective in his mid-thirties and by his forties (he's quite old now) he starts reading philosophy in earnest. Not just for intellectual interest but for the good of his soul. Now his bodily passions are less strong he feels a call to a new kind of integration. Sexual love had never been where he experienced his true self. It had no connection with the transcendent ground of all things. How could what we call sexuality carry such significance in a world in which sexual activity brought one so close to change, decay and death? Where the consequence of sex might so easily be an extra pregnancy, danger, disease? He comes to a point where he is simply ready to give up sexual relationships. He experiences a degree of relief. He will remain affectionate with his wife. Close friendships with men provide intellectual companionship and satisfaction. But as he prepares for death, he wants peace.

Sexuality Today as an Expression of Real Selfhood

On the whole we don't share his sexual pessimism. For us, sexuality is a soft-lit land of promise and disappointment. Most of us see our sexuality as a vital expression of our real selfhood whether or not we are in a sexual relationship. Even those positively committed to celibacy are encouraged to come to terms with their sexual identity and orientation.

Those who are in sexual relationships expect them to be fulfilling and are disappointed if they are not. We even hope that they will show us something of the divine. A poll conducted for the American magazine *Newsweek* in 1994 discovered that 26 per cent of those polled associated sexual activity with a sense of the sacred. Sex, for over a quarter of us, has become a channel of the transcendent.

The Struggle to Understand Sexuality Linked to Developing Issues in Christology

But early Christianity, like the Judaism from which it sprung, breathes the air of Platonized Stoicism. The passions, real as they are, are not where the true self resides. God does not really connect with this world of change and death; his incarnate Logos goes about robed in flesh, but still unlimited in his divine powers. Or does he? The first five centuries of Christian theology are fraught with the battle to discover how the unchanging, passionless God can really connect with human beings in the incarnation. And winding like a thread through the great christological debates – Docetism, Gnosticism, Arianism, Apollinarianism, Nestorianism – is the unasked question about the meaning of the flesh and the status of human desire.

In Gnosticism, for example, the Church is confronted with attempts to interpret the gospel through a mythology derived from Platonism. In the Gnostic system of Valentinus reality is all one; the divine *plerōma* is our source and our home, emanating outward from the depth of the divine. Creation occurs because of a disruption of the oneness of the one, caused by the sudden passion of Sophia for the unknowable depth of the Father's being. As the *plerōma* struggles to re-achieve harmony, Sophia's passion is cast out of the *plerōma* and becomes the seed of the material creation. Gnosticism was not only a form of theology. It was also Platonic spirituality. The journey back for the redeemed soul was a journey of contemplation. The one ascended to the one by abandoning desire. The Church resisted Gnosticism; but it still incorporated some of its assumptions. The ascent of the soul to the passionless one became a template for ascetic spirituality.

Origen Uses the Song of Songs to Describe the Soul as the Bride of Christ

Origen of Alexandria, the great Bible scholar of the third century, was the first to exploit erotic language to describe the ascent of the soul to God through stages of contemplation on Scripture. The soul, according to Origen, 'is led by a heavenly love and desire, and when once the beauty and the glory of the Word of God has been perceived, the soul falls in love with his splendour and by this receives from him some dart and wound of love' (Origen, 1979, p. 223). His commentary on the Song of Songs assumes that it is instruction for the soul from the heavenly bridegroom. The Song of Songs, in fact, is an erotic love song, containing no references to God at all. It would have been excluded from the Jewish canon had it not been for the impassioned pleading of Rabbi Akiba, who insisted on its divine inspiration and authority. Since then Jewish exegetes had interpreted the Song metaphorically as a celebration of the love of God for Israel, and Christian commentators before Origen followed their example; interpreting it as being about God and the new Israel, the Christian Church. Origen, however, while allowing this interpretation, also individualized the meaning of the Song, laying a foundation which would later bear fruit in many strands of Christian spirituality from Bernard of Clairvaux to the English Puritans of the seventeenth century.

The Legacy of Origen: The Place of Sexuality

Origen left us with a possibility and problem. For if he was right in seeing the Song of Songs as a metaphor of the passionate longing of the soul for God, then two possibilities are opened for the way in which we might understand human passion and sexual desire. Either we could argue that human desire has the potential to mirror the divine love, so bringing a degree of transcendental significance to human sexuality, or we could argue that the sheer intensity of the soul for the divine actually squeezes out and diminishes the significance of human passion.

Monasticism as the Purest Way to a Pure God

What I think settled the matter in the short term was the continuing tendency in early Christianity to understand God in Neo-Platonic terms. God remained Monad, ultimately unknowable. The incarnation was understood as the unfolding of the monad towards us in compassion and healing. But the final truth of God is singularity, and we mimic God best when we too exert our most strenuous efforts to become monads, monachoi, in other words, monks. Paul's urgent apocalypticism becomes the monks' longing for perfection, a solitary perfection which imitates a solitary God. There is compassion for the creatures, there is growth in charity and humility, but in the end the imagination assumes the journey home to God to be what the Neo-Platonic philosopher Plotinus would call 'a flight of the alone to the alone'.

Spirituality, then, is cosmic homesickness, the soul's sense of its own loss and distance, and its efforts to return from the land of unlikeness to its true home. God is the object of our greatest longing, God, in being God, is all-sufficient, needing nothing, not even our love. Contemplation and asceticism begin the journey back to participation in the divine mind. Sexuality, on the other hand, brings distraction, trouble, it is the cause of a heavy heart and a divided soul.

Augustine: The Conflict Confessed

With Augustine we reach the most beautifully expressed record of the conflict between prayer and sexuality that exists in Christian literature, a conflict resolved for Augustine in personal terms, which, while powerfully moving, are perhaps less revolutionary than the legacy of his mature thought.

We are at the end of the fourth century in the Western half of the Christianized Roman empire. Augustine, the rhetorician, philosopher, Christian convert and bishop, prays his life back to God in repentance and thanksgiving. His *Confessions* look back with shame over his childhood, youth and early manhood. He is a man who presents himself as having a high sexual drive and he writes with regret of the lusts of his youth. He also has a generous and expansive heart. He lives faithfully with a concubine. He loves his male friends. He rejects Christianity but finds himself drawn to the rather weird but influential and numerous sect of the Manichees. He learns from them that sex is evil and this keeps him from the inner circle of Manichean initiates. Instead he lives the divided life of the half believer, as a Manichee 'hearer' he is allowed to live chastely with his woman. Eventually he leaves the Manichees and is attracted to philosophy.

All the time he knows that the longing for God is in competition with his sexuality. Both can't win. It is one or the other. As he moves towards Neo-Platonism he feels the characteristic homesickness of the lost self for the one, and the lure of the asceticism which promises him freedom from the chains of sexual desire. His concubine is shipped back home to North Africa while his mother plans a suitable marriage for one of his proper social status. But the marriage is not to be. Augustine, like many before and after, is deeply impressed by that fourth-century best-seller which changed so many lives, Athanasius's *Life of Antony*. Tradition presents Antony as the first real Christian monk, the founder of a way of life which is absolute in its search for God. Augustine grasps the possibility of living a life of continence in imitation of the God who is pure and one and beyond the one.

Our tendency, when we read Augustine, is to move too quickly to that garden in Milan where he experiences the heartbreak of the will, and picks up the Bible at Romans and is converted to the Lord Jesus Christ, making no provision for the lusts of the flesh. But if we do so we miss what was an immensely important turning-point, not only for Augustine, but for all of us as we reflect on the conflict of Christian spirituality and sexuality.

Victorinus and the Trinity as Eternal Movement

That turning-point was the conversion to Christianity of one of the most eminent Neo-Platonic philosophers of the day, Marius Victorinus. It was Victorinus who realized that the Neo-Platonic pattern was, in the end, crushing to humanity. The God derived from Platonism is so all-sufficient that he is in the end only able to be everything. He cannot therefore love anything, for there is nothing for him to love. Though we long for unity with God, our highest love for God simply disappears into God's ineffable being.

Victorinus took a bold step when he saw that the human longing for God does not begin with us, but is a response to God's love. God's being is not static, but ec-static, movement, his being is not pure because it is void of desire, but because its very nature is desire. His very being is gift to us. This is the mystery of the life of the Trinity, an endless cycle of love as gift, in which to quote Louis Bouyer: 'the Father casts himself into the very being of the Son, who knows himself, recognising his Father as such, only in returning to him, not to be absorbed by him but to exult in the Spirit in their community of life, a life, Life itself, which is nothing but gift' (Bouyer, 1990, p. 204).

This is the Western version of *perichoresis*, the coinherence of the Greek fathers who perceived the Trinity as three interpenetrating orbs of infinite radiance, three suns, whose splendour spills over to embrace and contain the created world.

It was Victorinus who showed Augustine the way, who enabled him to see that the clamour of his heart for peace was a faint echo of God's original love for him. This was when Augustine really understood the incarnation. He had indeed, as he says in the *Confessions*, read all about the Word of God in Plato and the philosophers, but he did not read in their books that 'the Word became flesh and dwelt among us . . .'. With Victorinus's conversion he saw why the Word had to become flesh. Without the incarnation God cannot really reach us.

Consequences for Augustine

So what has this to do with sexuality? Not much, you might think, since the immediate outcome was that Augustine embraced celibacy with enthusiasm and went on to work out a doctrine of original sin which involved the transmission of the consequences of Adam's crime through sexual intercourse. He also suggested that if it had not been for original sin human reproduction would have taken place without the need for genital excitement.

The Trinity: A Context for Understanding Human Sexuality

But what Augustine received from Victorinus and passed on to us is a picture of God whose very being is active love, movement, desire. And this active love is both the life of the Trinity and also the life for which we are created.

What is then achieved in the trinitarian teaching of the fifth century is a way of looking at God which builds on, and even fulfils the insights of Judaism and Platonism, while at the same time going beyond them. It is a way of looking at God in which human sexuality could be mirrored positively and creatively, without our being bound by the misogynist traditionalism that still affects many of the world's societies and much conventional Christian teaching on the subject.

What Do We Learn of God and Sex from Trinitarian Teaching?

So what do we draw out of this trinitarian teaching? First, the Trinity is not sexualized. There is no compromise with the mysteries; Christianity neither invites nor permits us to worship Jung's phallus or the ear of corn. Sex is not the one holy secret mystery of the universe. There is no divine marriage within the Trinity, no Mr or

Mrs Yahweh. We don't worship a Father Mother God. When we call God 'Father' we call him by a personal name, not because it is a description of a sexual function.

Yet, nor is God to be understood simply as everything. God is not simply the totality of being to whom we return having shed our sexuality and become pure and one as God is. We are not linked to God's being by nature, poised to return to our ultimate source. The creativity of God moves outward, it is not static, but ec-static, always beyond itself. The divine mind dreams variety, difference and freedom. That serious playfulness that is God's creativity implants creativity in us. Human generativity and human culture are appropriately expressed in the emotional and bodily excitement of sexual relationships.

This is where the Stoic insistence on detachment meets the Christian requirement of active *agapē*, and not *agapē* only, but a Christian celebration of desire, *erōs* as a reflection in us of the plenitude of God's joy. In this sense, God is *plerōma*, the fullness of all things, and *erōs* and *agapē*, so often separated in us, in God comprise that 'love which moves the sun and the other stars'.

Within that, we may conclude there are a variety of vocations, a range of personal journeys. Those who work as spiritual directors, many of them celibate religious, are aware that variety is inevitable. They listen as prayerful Christians tell them of movements in and out of celibacy. Of God breaking a marriage as well as making one. Of homosexual love bringing individuals to a truthful mirroring of God's image in them. Of singleness that flowers unexpectedly. And because they know God is love, and love is both *agapē*, self-gift, and *erōs*, desire, they are disinclined, if they can see evidence of blessing, to make moralizing judgements about the intimate behaviour of those who seek their counsel.

I would conclude by saying that our sexuality is the playground in the school of prayer, for it is where we tumble over our greatest needs and hungers, where the possibility of erotic delight is revealed, the limitations of our self-love are exposed, and pride is purged. Because there is no tidiness in the Christian tradition; no ultimate exaltation of celibacy over marriage or marriage over celibacy; no possibility of a final repression of homosexual love; no sustainable matriarchy or patriarchy; our sexuality remains the place of great personal intensity where we are have the capacity to be most open and most closed to God because it is where we are most open and closed to one another. This is why it remains a place of trouble and torment and also, I believe, of the greatest earthly blessing and happiness. I think in the prosperous Western world, where so many of our material needs are taken care of, where on the whole there is peace, and death comes at the end of life for most people, it is in working through and living out our sexual identity and orientation that we are most likely to experience the shadow of Christ's cross and to wait within the life-giving paradox of the empty tomb. 'My desire is crucified' cried Ignatius of Antioch as he went to his martyrdom at the beginning of the Christian era. The word he used was *erōs*, and for Origen and those who followed him this meant, 'my love', and further still it meant, Christ, the passion of God and our hope of redemption.

References

Bouyer, L., *The Christian Mystery*. T. & T. Clark, Edinburgh, 1990.

Origen, *Prologue to the Commentary on the Song of Songs*, in *Origen: Selections*, ed. R. A. Greer. SPCK, London, 1979.

Studdert Kennedy, G. A., *The Unutterable Beauty*. Mowbray, London, 1983 (first published 1927).

Further Reading

Augustine, St, *Confessions*. Penguin, London, 1961.

Brown, P., *The Body and Society: Men, Women and Sexual Renunciation in Early Christianity*. Faber & Faber, London, 1989.

Coakley, S. (ed.), *Religion and the Body*. Cambridge University Press, Cambridge, 1997.

Hayes, M., Porter, W., and Tombs, D. (eds), *Religion and Sexuality*. Sheffield Academic Press, Sheffield, 1998.

Nelson, J., and Longfellow, S. (eds), *Sexuality and the Sacred: Sources for Theological Reflection*. Mowbray, London, 1994.

Slade, H., *Contemplative Intimacy*. Darton, Longman & Todd, London, 1977.

Thatcher, A., and Stewart, E. (eds), *Christian Perspectives on Sexuality and Gender*. Gracewing, Leominster, 1996.

CHAPTER EIGHT

Prayer and the Body

Sara Savage

Prayer and the body pair awkwardly. The networks of related concepts that these two terms ignite seem wholly opposed. I recently polled a church gathering for related terms. 'Prayer' evoked concepts such as angels, quiet, peace, holiness, eternity. 'Body' evoked concepts such as human, earthbound, sex, excitement, fatigue, mortality. Enmeshed, these networks screech like two gears grinding. Yet, despite this strained relationship, there are various ways in which prayer and the body can be related in Christian practice. I will discuss three here.

The Body as a Container for Prayer

At the most elementary level, our bodies are a necessary instrument for prayer. We need bodies in order to sit or kneel or stand to pray; we need brains in order to formulate our prayer. While praying, it is usually helpful to have the back erect, pulling up from the base of the spine, with the head loosely resting on top of the spine, as if a string is pulling upwards from the top of the head. This helps us to breathe through the nostrils, drawing our breath deeply from the diaphragm, and to release any tension held in the neck, shoulders and limbs. Soon our breathing and heart rate slow down, and our bodies relax. Yet we remain alert, free to explore the deeper issues that concern us. There is a good deal of evidence that brain activity changes in deep prayer; the brain is involved in a different, but therapeutic way of processing information. There is also survey evidence that the activity of prayer is good for physical health, as well as mental health, although any causal relationship between these is mostly likely to be complex. Praying produces mutually beneficial spin-offs between body and mind.

Meditative prayer in various world religions seeks to attain altered bodily and mental states. In Transcendental Meditation (TM), it is the altered, tranquil state that is sought. TM does not posit that there is a God to whom we pray; the focus is on the means, not the end. In hatha-yoga, the devotee practises a demanding range of physical disciplines (stretches, balances, deep breathing exercises, cleansing diets) as part of a physical pathway for spiritual aspirations. In Zen Buddhism, the contemplation of paradoxical statements so frustrates the human desire to understand and to control that the mind finally gives up, and is thereby one step nearer to the blissful nothingness of nirvana. The rocking back and forth in Jewish Hasidism, and the spinning dances of the whirling dervishes of the Sufi Islamic sect are also bodily practices which set out to achieve temporary alterations in bodily and cognitive processing. An extreme example is the use of mind-altering chemicals in some traditional (and modern) religions or sects.

With Christian prayer or meditation, altered states are seen as an occasional by-product, not as an end in themselves. The early Church fathers distanced themselves from the ecstatic practices of paganism and mystery religions: Christians are children of the light (daytime rationality), not children of the night. Communion with God in Christian prayer is possible through ordinary, rational states of consciousness as well as the more extraordinary, altered states sometimes reported with visions and religious experiences. Christianity has perhaps been more circumspect about claims to altered states as a desirable feature of prayer than have other religions, which has meant that Christianity has seemed to have less on 'offer' to people who wish to explore these aspects of prayer. These experiences are not as rare as we might think. They are described not only by Christianity's saints and mystics; religious experiences are also reported by around 30 per cent to 60 per cent of the UK adult population, according to two different methods of surveys, carried out by David Hay (Hay, 1990). The Toronto Blessing has attracted both fervent interest (as well as fervent opposition) among Christians because of the predominance of ecstatic and unusual bodily responses exhibited by adherents. Participants are convinced of the veracity of their religious experience; onlookers are perplexed, if not repelled, such is the awkward pairing of bodily manifestations in conjunction with prayer in Christian history.

With the more usual, restrained approach to prayer in Christian practice, the body is seen as a necessary instrument or container for prayer, yet one which can allow us to transcend the limits of the body, and our normal sense of our habitation in time and space. It is as if the body co-operates with the longing of the soul to transcend its own limitations in time and space, and to reach out and connect with the divine. The most usual Christian disciplines employ quietness, stillness, and a religious focus, such as Scripture readings, a cross, or a stained glass window, to facilitate a 'forgetting' of the body as part of the spiritual quest. This is the most common way we put together these two apparently contradictory terms of the body and prayer. We could call this prayer in spite of the body, albeit with the help of the body.

Implicitly, this approach to prayer relies on a certain understanding of the relationship of soul or spirit to the physical realm. There is a long standing antipathy in the Church towards the body and bodily movement. This is based, not so much on Scripture, but on certain strands of Greek philosophy. The philosophers Pythagoras, Plato and Plotinus thought of the body as inherently corrupt, the enemy of the soul. The impact of the body on the soul gives rise to evil. Death was seen as a happy release from the prison or tomb of the body. Plotinus, whose Neo-Platonism was adopted into Christian thinking, spoke of the soul as being 'immersed in filth and daubed with the mud of the body'; 'The nature of the body, in that it partakes of matter, is an evil thing . . . a hindrance to the soul in its proper act' (Plotinus, quoted in Davies, 1984, p. 86). The problem with the body was its materiality. The Greek world-view was divided between the realm of the 'ideal' on the one hand, as in Platonic ideal forms, pure mathematics, and geometry, and the material world on the other. The ideal forms were thought of as the ultimate, eternal realities of the universe. In contrast, the material world was understood as the imperfect, decaying, transient expression of the ideal. The human body was an exemplar of this transience and corruptibility. The religious quest became a never ending battle against the 'flesh', which was equated with the physical body.

Attitudes towards the body found their way into Christian liturgy via the science of rhetoric. The rules of rhetoric, first expounded by Cicero, and later taken up by the Church fathers, elevated the spirit over the material, and recommend a minimum of gesture or movement. From antiquity down to the Middle Ages, the ideal of godlike immobility was preferred to bodily movement. Immobility came to signify the 'spirit'. An absence of movement became the signifier of the spiritual. God was pictured as impassable, the unmoved mover, the One who is beyond.

Descartes further developed this separation between soul (mind) and body, adding another layer of the dualism deeply incorporated into our thinking today. The philosopher Gilbert Ryle describes the outlines of the layperson's 'official doctrine' of the human mind. This taken-for-granted theory of mind goes like this: 'The human being consists of two distinct, yet separate kinds of thing: the body and the soul, or mind. The body acts as a host or receptacle for the mind, or perhaps even as a prison from which liberation may be sought through spiritual advancement or death' (Davies, 1983, p. 79). Ryle calls this explanation of mind 'the ghost in the machine': the mind is the ghostly substance, the physical brain is the machine.

The fundamental error of this kind of dualism is to consider the mind as different in substance from the body (and brain). More recent scientific paradigms provide a new way of thinking about the relation of the mind to the body. This can be better understood as the relation between the plot of a novel to letters of the alphabet, or a Beethoven symphony to the notes of a musical score. They denote, not two different substances, but different concepts drawn from different levels of organization. The high-level concept of the mind, with its incredible complexity, is just as 'real' as the low-level bodily/brain structures that support it. Mind (or soul) needs to be understood holistically. Mind is better understood as the achievement of the body's supporting structures, just as a Beethoven symphony is the achievement of the separate notes that make it up, rather than a ghostly substance inhabiting it.

It is not necessary to think of the body as something different from and inferior to the mind, or as a hindrance to be overcome. It is more in line with current thinking to see the body and brain as supporting the higher cognitive activities. When liberated from the dualist model, there is good argument for a more active use of the body in prayer.

Prayer Using the Bodily Senses: Ignatian Prayer

St Ignatius Loyola taught his followers to engage their imaginations and their five senses in prayer. Living in sixteenth-century Spain during the Counter Reformation, Ignatius did not endear himself to the Inquisition authorities with his method. Ignatian prayer contrasts with the more usual practice in religious life which eschewed sense perception or any excitement due to 'worldliness'. For example, St Teresa of Avila would not allow her cloistered nuns to look out their carriage window en route to another convent, lest they be distracted from their interior focus on God. With the *Spiritual Exercises*, Ignatius provided his followers with a spirituality that underscored the outward looking, missionary zeal of the Jesuit order he founded.

Rather than turning away from the created world, prayer with the senses and imagination makes use of the created world. Everything is fair game; the sights, sounds and smells of everyday life are grist to the mill. The technique Ignatius taught is simply to insert yourself into a Gospel account or passage of Scripture. Using the imagination, the person praying lives out the story, perhaps as an observer, or even in the first person, imagining the sights, the sounds, the smells, and the action of the scene. Ignatian prayer employs that rich playground, the imagination, which brings together aspects of reality and fantasy. The psychologist D. W. Winnicott speaks of the imagination as an arena where we can actively formulate creative solutions to life's problems, just as a child who clings to his or her teddy-bear creatively internalizes the sense of security provided by a caring mother. Like children with teddy-bears, who thus provide themselves with the courage to go out into the real world, when we use our imagination in prayer, we can become active collaborators in our own transformation.

For example, Ignatius recommended that, when at meals, his followers should imagine Jesus eating and drinking with his disciples; they should 'see' the food, 'smell' the smells, and 'taste' the tastes, visualizing the way Christ enjoyed the food and how he shared in the fellowship of eating with his disciples. Ignatius wisely considered this sort of reframing to be a more effective way of dealing with the sins of gluttony and greed, in contrast to endless rounds of self-mortification in the private pursuit of personal sanctity. Pragmatically speaking, such reframing empowered Ignatius' followers for active service, rather than rendering them exhausted through self-denial.

Using our senses and imagination also helps us in developing social knowledge, knowledge of other persons. This can happen to us as we insert ourselves into the Gospel accounts. We get to know others by interacting with them, using our senses to observe them, eventually developing an internal image of that person based on our real life interactions with them. It seems that we come to know God as a person in ways which implicitly rely on the normal psychological processes we employ in knowing other human beings: through being part of an unfolding narrative that reveals who that other person is. The *Spiritual Exercises* implicitly rely on such processes. As Jesus, the fully human Son of God, has made himself available to the human senses of the disciples in history, we too can share in that experience with the help of our imagination, and the quickening presence of the Holy Spirit. Knowing another person also relies on a degree of self-knowledge. This too increases when I insert myself into a Gospel story. As I observe, in my imagination, Jesus' encounter with Zacchaeus up in the tree, I am struck by the surprising way Christ overturns the crowd's expectations concerning who is worthy to be his host for the night. As one of the crowd, I am also surprised by my own reaction of jealousy and resentment, as I watch a swindler like Zacchaeus get something I don't think he deserves.

Prayer with the Body

Here, we pray actively *with* our physical body through movement. Throughout Scripture, a view emerges of human beings as a body–spirit unity, rather than the idea of a physical, bodily container housing an immortal soul (a Greek, rather than a Hebrew idea). Consistent with a holistic picture of the human person, Scripture exhorts us to love God with all our mind, with all our heart, with all our soul and with all our strength. As body–spirit beings, it is natural that our prayer is both bodily and spiritual. A simple illustration of praying with the body is the Jewish gesture of prayer: hands outstretched, supplicating, open, waiting to receive an answer. Many liturgical gestures and practices (such as kneeling, receiving the sacraments, going on pilgrimage) give worshippers an opportunity to act out, as well as to think, their devotions.

Religious practices can however, over time, become emptied of their meaning, or at least lose some of their impact. We may need to go beyond traditional ways of moving our prayers and invent new ways. For example, if I am praying on my own, I might physically act out my prayer like a little drama. I might move out of how I am feeling in order to speak to God about my current state. If I am feeling depressed, I might flop on the floor or curl myself up into a ball. Through this, I am revealing how I feel, both to myself and to God. I might feel the need to reach out to a symbol of Christ's presence, such as a cross or an icon. These movements can open me up to God in a new honesty, and engage me actively as I seek transformation of my problems. If I am praying for someone else, perhaps for someone buried in a recent earthquake, I might lie down on the floor in a twisted position, imagining tons of rubble over me. The fear, the shock, the physical pain of crushed bones, the torment of trying to get enough air through the rubble, the thirst and the probability of never being found fill me with desperation. My empathy with this imagined person fuels my prayer. This uncomfortably real compassion for the victims of the earthquake makes me realize that great haste is needed in the rescue effort. I pray for this, and being burdened by it, perhaps I even make a generous donation to the relief agencies involved. Through active physical involvement with our prayers we can become part of the answer to our own prayer, part of the arsenal that is now at God's disposal to fashion the real world.

A major benefit from praying this way is that I am becoming fully involved in my prayer. Most importantly, I am activating my will. As conscious agents in this world, we cannot move our body unless we will to do so. When moving, either I will need to align myself with the prayer I am acting out, or else I will experience an uncomfortable sense of dissonance. My true intentions become clear to me, thus fulfilling one of the functions of prayer: reflection upon our own desires and intentions in the light of Christ's presence (see the chapter by Fraser Watts in this volume). As I bring into my awareness my thoughts, feelings, and desires, I become able, and responsible, with God's help, to do something about them.

Given these benefits, why then, do we not engage in this sort of praying with the body more often? Firstly, it appears not to be part of our Christian tradition. The Church has tended throughout the ages to be hostile to grass-roots expressions of worship in movement and dance. However, further back, movement and dance can be seen as an intrinsic part of our Judeo-Christian heritage. The Old Testament in particular makes numerous references to dance as a part of worship in Israel. Dance in worship is a cultural practice so universal in human history that it would have been surprising had dance not been part of worship in Israel. In a culture which did not emphasize a clear body–soul division, movement functioned as a form of spiritual communication. Note the prophets Isaiah and Ezekiel acting out the coming invasion of Israel and Jerusalem, respectively, living out the appalling consequences through symbolic actions. Jesus enacted his prayer for us during the Last Supper; he broke the bread and shared out the wine as a physically acted-out symbol, transforming his forthcoming passion into a life-giving sacrament. However, as we have already seen, the early Church fathers saw the need to distance themselves from the pagan practices surrounding the growing Church, and this combined with prevailing philosophic ideas that accorded with stillness, rather than movement, as a marker of spirituality.

Another reason why we rarely engage in this form of prayer is that using our bodies in prayer or worship exposes us to our human vulnerability. Our feelings of anger, fear, sadness or guilt all find their way into our bodies; we feel them in our bodies, and our bodies bear their brunt through stress-related illnesses. Some theorists believe that emotions are not only stored in our memory, they are stored kinaesthetically, in the muscles and organs of our physical bodies. To move out our bodies in prayer can activate those sleeping lions, a danger early monastic orders sought to avoid by forbidding members of religious orders to move in spontaneous, individual ways.

A third reason is Christianity's uneasy relationship with sexuality. This is more fully elucidated in the chapter on 'Prayer and Sexuality' by Angela Tilby in this volume. The Platonic and Stoic imprint on

Christianity cast the spiritual quest as an escape from physicality, from passion, from need, from movement, from sexuality. With this legacy, our bodies do not seem holy enough, or spiritual enough, to bring into God's presence. So we tend to leave our physicality, and our sexuality, outside our church doors.

This is not to suggest that we should swing to an opposite extreme and to indulge or sentimentalize the human body. We do have an 'animal' nature. Archaeological evidence to date indicates that the modern human frame evolved long before our human brain. Our humanoid ancestors became upright, bipedal, with skilful tool-making hands, with bodies similarly proportioned to the ones we see today, long before the brain capacity of *Homo sapiens* developed. One archaeologist described it thus: if you were walking in the savannah in Africa, from a distance, you would have recognized our humanoid ancestor as one of us. Their frame was just like ours, although taller and stronger than most of our athletes today. Not until you got closer would you have realized that you were looking into the eyes, not of a fellow human being, but of a very efficient hunting animal.

Our bodies are our primitive heritage. The Freudian view of the unconscious as a vast repository of powerful sexual and aggressive drives paints a somewhat pessimistic view of human nature that seems in accord with our tendency to fear and denigrate the physical aspects of our being. Freud was right in claiming, however, that denying the sexual drive in an attempt to emulate holiness generally backfires. In this vein, it is important that we do not mistake our animal nature for something inherently evil, and thus try to repress it, and split ourselves off from it. Rather, our bodies and our physical needs are morally neutral. Morality depends on how we use the totality of our capacities as human beings. If we think of our own bodies as animalistic in an evil sense, we are in danger of disowning this part of ourselves, and projecting on to others what we disown in ourselves. To view our bodies as an object that needs aggressive control can give us permission to do the same to others, to see them as body-objects. A feature of human cruelty is the tendency to see the 'enemy' in less than human terms. We view them only as body-objects, because that is all we can 'see'.

Thus, how we understand our body is important for moral action, as well as for our prayer and worship. Morality has to do with accurate perception and thinking. Self-deceptive practices, such as disowning one's body or emotions, do not improve moral behaviour, but rather impair it. As long as we can separate ourselves from our own bodies, we can treat others simply as body-objects. The worldwide Church calls itself the family of God; indeed this is an invitation extended to all humanity. What marks out family relationships from other human relationships is not only their permanence and intimacy, but a deep familiarity with bodily needs. Family life revolves around care for the body. The raising of children, having sex, eating, caring for the ill and ageing are all provinces of the family. In the sphere of the family, we accept the physicality of our own kin without dismissing their spiritual nature, and yet we find it difficult to extend this holistic concern to the family of God, and even more difficult to extend to our 'enemy'.

Layered upon these ways of thinking about the body are our own contemporary attitudes. As never before, the body has assumed enormous importance, but in an oddly ambivalent way. Bodies are highly valued as long as they are sleek, athletic, young, beautiful, and sexually alluring. For some, the result of aspiring to these goals is anorexia; then, ironically, the desire to become sexually alluring ends up turning into a pathological desire to look pre-pubescent. The flip-side of body-worship is self-revulsion for the majority of people who do not attain Hollywood standards. The only way to escape self-condemnation (and indeed social discrimination, for both short and fat people are actively discriminated against in the marketplace) is incessant dieting or other efforts at self-improvement. The effort to sustain such a regime is often punctuated by bouts of self-indulgence, made all the more likely by continuous advertisements for fast foods. Both the fast food and the dieting/exercise industries are kept in business by this symbiotic relationship. We are enthralled, even enslaved by our bodies, but not because we actually like them. How difficult, and how liberating to 'present your bodies as a living sacrifice, holy and acceptable to God, which is your spiritual worship' (Romans 12.1). Our physical bodies are included in our relationship with God; and our obsessions about them can be disciplined through this reframing.

Scripture employs a range of metaphors depicting our relationship with God in increasing levels of intimacy. At the most basic level, we are the clay, and he is the potter. God is in relationship to us at the level where we are merely part of material creation. With compassion, he remembers that we are but dust. On a more evolved, animal level, we are the sheep of his pasture, and he is the shepherd. Although sheep are rather dumb animals, and none too clean, the sheep recognize the shepherd's voice, and the shepherd calls each one by name. On the human level, we are called slaves and servants, of whom he is the Master. But Jesus prefers to call us friends, so that we can know what the Master is doing, and actively collaborate with him in his work. Further, we are children of God and he is our Father. Most intimate still, we are his beloved, his bride, and he is the bridegroom who has sacrificed everything for the sake of winning her back to himself. With increasing intimacy comes increasing autonomy.

In all aspects of our being, we are loved by God. As his bride, we are grounded in the humility of our material and animal nature. Although we respond to God's upward calling, we cannot disown our embodied selves, because God does not disown our embodied selves, nor his own. Jesus did not simply shed his physical body after the resurrection. In a mysteriously transformed state, this physicality is now part of the Godhead.

We have often lost sight of this. So far, we have seen how some of the early Christian fathers, immured in the thinking of their day, underestimated the relational, passionate nature of the Triune God. In more modern times, we have also tended to overlook our own relational nature. 'Object Relations' theorists, such as D. Winnicott, H. Guntrip and R. Fairbairn, argue that Freud underestimated the importance of relationship for human beings, and exaggerated the importance of the gratification of urges and instincts. What we really seek is another 'object', a person outside of ourselves. What the infant seeks is not so much the oral satisfaction of suckling the breast, but a relationship with a mother or carer who confers a sense of being upon the infant as she lovingly returns the baby's gaze. We are relational beings, and we seek, and are sought by, a relational Triune God.

The object of prayer is relationship. Relationship is inter-subjective, and involves both a knowing of the other and a knowing of ourselves. Praying with the body, whether it be through simple gestures such as the raising of one's hands, or touching a symbol of Christ's presence, or in the physical acting out of prayers, or in extending those physical expressions to the fullness of the art of dance, we are focusing our wills, and bringing into our prayer all that we are in order to know ourselves, and to know Christ.

Conclusion

We began this chapter with an image of grinding gears; the discordant sound of opposed networks of terms. I now move to a more harmonious image of wheels within wheels, like the vision described by Ezekiel. Rather than grating against each other, each of the three approaches to integrating prayer and the body can enrich the others. The first, the body as container for prayer, can be pictured as the outer wheel. With this sort of prayer we can connect with God in his transcendence; the God who is timeless, infinite, and beyond even our most enlightened concepts of him. Our physical body co-operates with this quest, and through discipline and quietness, allows the mind to transcend the constraints of our perception of time and space in order to connect spirit to spirit. The riches of this aspect of our Christian heritage are inexpressible.

The second, Ignatian prayer, prayer with the help of the body's senses, and the third, praying actively with the body, pictured as wheels within wheels, become progressively more intimate with our own humanity, and Christ's. As we engage with who we are through our senses, imaginations, emotions and bodies, we can connect with God in his immanence, in Christ's human incarnation, and all that this means for the redemption of ourselves as body/spirits. My conclusion is, simply, why not practise all three ways of praying? Why not embark on the journey of knowing God in both his transcendence and his immanence? This is our Judeo-Christian heritage, which we have a right to reclaim.

References

Davies, J. G., *Liturgical Dance: An Historical, Theological and Practical Handbook.* SCM Press, London, 1984.

Davies, P., *God and the New Physics.* Dent, London, 1983.

Hay, D., *Religious Experience Today: Studying the Facts.* Mowbray, London, 1990.

Further Reading

For the therapeutic uses of movement and dance in prayer and worship:

Blogg, M., *Healing in the Dance*. Kingsway Publications, Eastbourne, 1988.

A more in-depth look at the history and theological implications of the Church's response to movement and dance, and the continuance of liturgical dance through the ages:

Davies, J. G., *Liturgical Dance: An Historical, Theological and Practical Handbook*. SCM Press, London, 1984.

For a discussion of emotions, and the 'religious refusal of the body':

Davis, C., *Body as Spirit: The Nature of Religious Feeling*. Hodder & Stoughton, London, 1976.

For the original exercises in prayer using the imagination and senses:

Ganss, G. (ed.), *Ignatius Loyola: The Spiritual Exercises and Selected Works*. Paulist Press, New York, 1991.

For a modern introduction to Ignatian spirituality:

Lonsdale, D., *Eyes to See, Ears to Hear: An Introduction to Ignatian Spirituality*. Darton, Longman & Todd, London, 1990.

For practical advice on beginning to use movement in worship, also a fascinating glimpse of the history of dance in church:

Randall, J., *In Him We Move*. Solway, Carlisle, 1999.

A chapter that expands on the psychological, sociological and theological implications of viewing the incarnation through the art of dance:

Savage, S., 'Through Dance: Fully Human Fully Alive', in J. Begbie (ed.), *Beholding the Glory: Incarnation through the Arts*. Darton, Longman & Todd, London, 2000.

Acknowledgements

Permission to use the following extracts has been kindly granted by the copyright holders. We have made our best endeavour to track all sources, but if there are any errors or omissions, we will be pleased to correct them at reprint.

Heaney, S., 'St Kevin and the Blackbird', from *Opened Ground: Selected Poems, 1966–1996.* Copyright © 1998 Seamus Heaney. Faber & Faber (1998), and Farrar, Straus and Giroux, LLC.

Southwell, Lady Anne, 'Precept 4', from *The Southwell-Sibthorpe Commonplace Book*, ed. J. Klene. Medieval and Renaissance Texts and Studies (1997), pp. 151–2.

Studdert Kennedy, G. A., 'Temptation', from *The Unutterable Beauty*, © G. A. Studdert Kennedy. Mowbray (1983).

Witherspoon, A. and Warnke, F. (eds), *Seventeenth-Century Prose and Poetry*, 2nd edn. Harcourt Brace and World (1963).